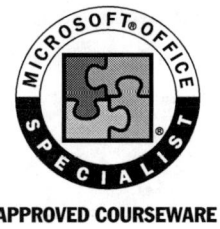

INSTRUCTOR-LED TRAINING

Microsoft®

MICROSOFT® OFFICE SPECIALIST

APPROVED COURSEWARE

GW01549341

Step by Step Courseware

Microsoft® Office XP

Microsoft®

Word

Version 2002

Core Skills Student Guide

PUBLISHED BY
ITS-Feda Ltd under licence from Microsoft Press
ITS-Feda Ltd is a Division of Reading College and School of Arts & Design
Coombe Lodge
Blagdon, Bristol, BS40 7RG,UK

Printed and bound in the UK by Basingstoke Press.

ISBN 1-904644-00-7

1 2 3 4 5 6 7 8 9   QWT   6 5 4 3 2 1 0

Microsoft Press books are available through booksellers and distributors worldwide. For further information about International editions contact your local Microsoft Corporation Office or contact Microsoft Press International directly at fax (425) 936-7329 or visit the Microsoft Press web site at mspress.Microsoft.com.
For further details of materials available from ITS-Feda Ltd please fax (44) 1761 461230 or visit www.itservices.org.uk. For comments regarding these materials please contact *books@itservices.org.uk.*

FrontPage Microsoft, MS-DOS, NetMeeting, Outlook, PowerPoint, SharePoint, Visual Basic, Windows and Windows NT are either registered trademarks or trademarks of Microsoft Corporation and /or other countries. Other product and company names mentioned herein may be the trademarks of their respective owners.

The example companies, organizations, products, domain names, e-mail addresses, logos, people, places and events depicted herein are fictitious. No association with any real company, organization, product, domain names, e-mail addresses, logos, people, places or events is intended or should be inferred.

Acknowledgements
Original Material

For Perspection Inc.
Managing Editors: Marjorie Hunt and Steve Johnson
Authors: Jane Pedicini, Jill Batistack, and Ed Dille
Development Editor: Lisa Ruffolo
Production Editor: Tracey Teyler, Beth Teyler and Virginia Felix-Simmons
Copy Editor: Lisa Ruffolo
Technical Editors: Kirsty Thielen and Melinda Lankford

For Microsoft Press
Acquisitions Editor: Kong Cheung

Revision to Instructor Led

For TESI Automazione srl
Managing Editor: Sebastiano Certo
Project Manager: Elisa Donzella
Technical Editor: Vito Burgì
Mous Master Instructor: Roberto Ferraù and Antonino Terranova
Production Team: Elio Di Mauro, Valerio Mirabella and Josephine Casaccio.

ITS-Feda Ltd
Project Manager: Penny Price
Technical Authors: G.E.T. I.T. Solutions Ltd

Contents

Course Overview

Welcome to the *Office Specialist XP Courseware* series for Microsoft Office 2002. This series facilitates classroom learning, letting students develop competence and confidence in using an Office application or operating system software. In completing courses taught with *Office Specialist XP Courseware,* students learn to use the software productively and discover how to make the software work for them. This series addresses core-level and expert-level skills in Microsoft Word 2002, Microsoft Excel 2002, Microsoft Access 2002, Microsoft Outlook 2002 and Microsoft FrontPage 2002. The *Office Specialist XP Courseware* series includes only one level for Microsoft PowerPoint 2002 called *comprehensive* and *Windows XP*.

The *Office Specialist XP Courseware* series provides:

- Task-based, results-oriented learning strategies.

- Exercises based on business scenarios.

- Complete preparation for Office Specialist certification.

- Attractive student guides with full-featured lessons.

- Lessons with accurate, logical and sequential instructions.

- Comprehensive coverage of skills from the basic to the expert level.

- A CD-ROM with practice files.

A Task-Based Approach Using Business Scenarios

The *Office Specialist XP Courseware* series builds on the strengths of the time-tested approach that Microsoft developed and refined for its Office Specialist XP series. Even though the Office Specialist XP series was created for self-paced training, instructors have long used it in the classroom. For the first time, this popular series has been adapted specifically for the classroom environment. By studying with a task-based approach, students learn more than just the features of the software. They learn how to accomplish real-world tasks so that they can immediately increase their productivity using the software application.

The lessons are based on tasks that students might encounter in the everyday work world. This approach allows students to quickly see the relevance of the training. The task-based focus is woven throughout the series, including lesson organization within each unit, lesson titles and scenarios chosen for practice files.

An Integrated Approach for Training

The *Office Specialist XP Courseware* series distinguishes itself from other series on the market with its consistent delivery and completely integrated approach to learning. With the addition of the *Office Specialist XP Courseware* series, which supports classroom instruction, the *Office Specialist XP* training suite now provides a flexible and unified training solution.

Preparation for Office Specialist Certification

This series has been certified as approved courseware for the Office Specialist certification program. Students who have completed this training are prepared to take the related Office Specialist exam. By passing the exam for a particular Office application, students demonstrate proficiency in that application to their employers or prospective employers. Exams are offered at participating test centres. For more information, see *www.microsoft.com/OfficeSpecialist*.

A Sound Instructional Foundation

All products in the *Office Specialist XP Courseware* series apply the same instructional strategies, closely adhering to adult instructional techniques and reliable adult learning principles. Lessons in the *Office Specialist XP Courseware* series are presented in a logical, easy-to-follow format, helping the student find information quickly and learn as efficiently as possible. To facilitate the learning process, each lesson follows a consistent structure.

Designed for Optimal Learning

The following "Lesson Features" section shows how the colourful and highly visual series design makes it easy for students to see what to read and what to do when practicing new skills.

Lessons break training into easily assimilated sessions. Each lesson is self- contained and lessons can be taught in sequences other than the one presented in the table of contents. Sample files for the lessons don't depend on completion of other lessons. Sample files within a lesson assume only that students are working sequentially through a complete lesson.

The *Office Specialist XP Courseware* series features:

- **Lesson objectives**. Objectives clearly state the instructional goals for each lesson so that students understand what skills they will master. Each lesson objective is covered in its own section and each section or topic in the lesson is covered in a consistent way. Lesson objectives preview the lesson structure, helping students grasp key information and prepare for learning skills.

- **Informational text for each topic**. For each objective, the lesson provides easy-to-read, technique-focused information.

- **Hands-on practice**. Numbered steps give detailed, step-by-step instructions to help students learn skills. The steps also show results and screen images to match what students should see on their computer screens. Student and instructor CDs contain sample files used for each lesson.

- **Full-colour illustrations in colour student guides**. Illustrated screen images give visual feedback to students as they work through exercises. The images reinforce key concepts, provide visual clues about the steps and bolster students' confidence by giving them something to check their progress against.

- **Office Specialist icon**. Each section or sidebar that covers an Office Specialist certification objective has an Office Specialist icon in the margin at the beginning of the section. The number of the certification objective is also listed.

- **Tips**. Helpful hints and alternate ways to accomplish tasks are located throughout the lesson text.

- **Important**. If there is something to watch out for or something to avoid, this information is added to the lesson and indicated with this heading.

- **Margin notes**. Margin notes (grey background) contain parenthetical topics or additional information that students might find interesting.

- **Button images in the margin**. When the text instructs students to click a particular button, an image of the button and its label appear in the margin.

- **Glossary.** Terms with which you might not be familiar are defined in the glossary in the back of this guide. Terms in the glossary appear in boldface type within the lesson and are defined upon their first use within lessons.

- **Quick Quiz**. You can use the short-answer quick quiz questions to test or reinforce your understanding of key topics within the lesson.

- **Quick Reference**. A complete summary of steps for tasks taught in each lesson is available in the back of the guide. This is often the feature that students find most useful when they return to their workplaces. The expert-level guides include the references from the core-level guides so that you can review or refresh basic and advanced skills on your own whenever necessary.

- **Index**. Student guides are completely indexed. All glossary terms and application features appear in the index.

Conventions and Features

This manual uses special forms, symbols and heading conventions to highlight important information or to call your attention to special steps. For more information about the features available in each lesson, refer to the "Course Overview" section.

Convention	Meaning
1 **2**	Numbered steps guide you through hands-on exercises in each topic.
●	A round bullet indicates an exercise that has only one step.
(CD icon)	This icon at the beginning of a lesson lists the files that the lesson will use and explains any file preparation that needs to take place before starting the lesson.
FileName (CD icon)	Practice files that you'll need to use in a topic's procedure are shown above the CD icon.
(Microsoft Office Specialist icon) W2002-3-2	This icon indicates a section that covers a Microsoft Office Specialist exam objective. The numbers above the icon refer to the specific Microsoft Office Specialist objective.
new for **Office**XP	This icon indicates a new or greatly improved feature in this version of Microsoft Word.
tip	This section provides a helpful hint or shortcut that makes working through a task easier.
important	This section points out information that you need to know to complete the procedure.

Convention	Meaning
troubleshooting	This section shows you how to fix a common problem.
Save 💾	When a button is referenced in a topic, a picture of the button appears in the margin area with a label.
Ctrl + End	A plus sign (+) between two key names means that you must hold down the first key while you press the other key. For example, "Press Ctrl + End" means that you hold down the Ctrl key while you press End.
Boldface	Program features that you click or press, terms that are explained in the glossary at the end of the book and the text that you are supposed to type appear in boldface type.
Practice files	All files that you need to practice the new skills taught in the lesson are located on the CD that is provided with each student guide. Instructions for installing the practice files are in the "Using the Book's CD" section near the beginning of the student guides.
Glossary	The glossary helps you to understand key terms. Terms that are defined in the glossary are shown in boldface type text in the lesson.
Margin notes	The notes contain additional information that might be useful to you.

Using the Book's CD

The CD-ROM included with this student guide contains the practice files that you'll use to perform the exercises in the books. By using the practice files, you won't waste time creating the samples used in the lessons and you can concentrate on learning how to use Microsoft Word 2002.

important

This book does not contain the Word 2002 software. You should purchase and install that program before using this book.

System Requirements

- **Computer/Processor**

  Computer with a Pentium 133-megahertz (MHz) or higher processor

- **Memory**

  RAM requirements depend on the operating system used:

  - **Windows 98, or Windows 98 Second Edition**

    24 MB of RAM plus an additional 8 MB of RAM for each Office program (such as Microsoft Word) running simultaneously

  - **Windows Me, or Microsoft Windows NT**

    32 MB of RAM plus an additional 8 MB of RAM for each Office program (such as Microsoft Word) running simultaneously

  - **Windows 2000 Professional**

    64 MB of RAM plus an additional 8 MB of RAM for each Office program (such as Microsoft Word) running simultaneously

- **Hard Disk**

  Hard disk space requirements will vary depending on configuration; custom installation choices may require more or less hard disk space.

245 MB of available hard disk space with 115 MB on the hard disk where the operating system is installed. (Users without Windows 2000, Windows Me, or Office 2000 Service Release 1 [SR-1] require an extra 50 MB of hard disk space for System Files Update.)

An additional 6 MB of hard disk space is required for installing the practice files.

■ **Operating System**

Windows 98, Windows 98 Second Edition, Windows Millennium Edition (Windows Me), Windows NT 4.0 with Service Pack 6 (SP6) or later, or Windows 2000 or later. (On systems running Windows NT 4.0 with SP6, Microsoft Internet Explorer must be upgraded to at least version 4.01 with SP1.)

■ **Drive**

CD-ROM drive

■ **Display**

Super VGA (800 × 600) or higher-resolution monitor with 256 colours

■ **Peripherals**

Microsoft Mouse, Microsoft IntelliMouse, or compatible pointing device

■ **Software**

Microsoft Word 2002, Microsoft Excel 2002, Microsoft Outlook 2002 and Microsoft Internet Explorer 5 or later

Installing the Practice Files

You need to install the practice files on your hard disk before you use them in the lessons' exercises. Follow these steps to prepare the CD's files for your use:

1   Insert the CD-ROM into the CD-ROM drive of your computer.

A menu screen appears

troubleshooting

If the menu screen does not appear, start Windows Explorer. In the left pane, locate the icon for your CD-ROM and click this icon. In the right pane, double-click the **StartCD** file.

2   Click **Install Practice Files**.

3   Click **OK** in the initial message box.

4 If you want to install the practice files to a location other than the default folder (C:\SBS\Word), click the **Change Folder** button, select the new drive and path and then click **OK**.

5 Click the **Continue** button to install the selected practice files.

6 After the practice files have been installed, click **OK**.

Within the installation folder are subfolders for each lesson in the book.

7 Remove the CD-ROM from the CD-ROM drive and return it to the envelope at the back of the book.

Using the Practice Files

Each lesson's introduction lists the files that are needed for that lesson and explains any file preparation that you need to take care of before you start working through the lesson.

OpenDoc

Each topic in the lesson explains how and when to use any practice files. The files that you'll need are indicated in the margin at the beginning of the procedure above the CD icon:

The following table lists each **Core** lesson's practice files.

Lesson	Folder	Files
1	CreatingDoc	EditDoc, ExistDoc, OpenDoc and ReplaceText
2	FormattingText	FormatText, FormatAuto, FormatPara and CreateList
3	FormattingDoc	FormatPage and FormatStyle
4	ProofingPrint	SpellCheck and PreviewPrint
5	AddingTables	CreateTable, FormatTable and CreateColumn
6	Drawing	OrgChart, InsertPics Gardenco and WordArt
7	Charting	AddChart and ModChart
8	Collaborating	CompareMerge, Merge1, Merge2 and RevComment
9	WorkingWeb	CreateWeb and OtherLogos

The following table lists each **Expert** lesson's practice files

Lesson	Folder	Files
1	FormattingText	CreateList
2	FormattingDoc	FormatPage and FormatStyle
3	AddingTables	CreateTable, DataTable and InsertTable
4	Drawing	AlignPics
5	Charting	ImportData and FileImport
6	Collaborating	TrackChange, CompareMerge, Merge1, Merge2, ProtectDoc, Attach1, Attach2 and Send
7	WorkingWeb	CreateWeb, OtherLogos, ModWebDoc, WebSignature and AddSignature
8	Customising	CustomMenu, CustomToolbar, RecordMacro and ModifyMacro
9	MerginData	FormLetter, NewFormLtr, FinalFormLtr, MergeLtr, Data, Data2 and Data3
10	CreatingForms	CreateForm and UseForm
11	CreatingNotes	Footnote, ReviseNotes, Bookmark and Master
12	CreatingToc	TabContents, MarkEntry and CreateIndex

Uninstalling the Practice Files

After you finish working through this book, you should uninstall the practice files to free up hard disk space.

1   On the Windows taskbar, click the **Start** button, point to **Settings** and then click **Control Panel**.

2   Double-click the **Add/Remove Programs** icon

3   **In the list of installed programs, click Microsoft Word 2002 SBS Files** and then click **Add/Remove**. (If you're using Windows 2000 Professional, click the **Remove** or **Change/Remove** button.)

4   Click **Yes** when the confirmation dialog box appears.

tip

If you need additional help installing or uninstalling the practice files, please see the section "Getting Help" earlier in this book. Microsoft's product support does not provide support for this book or its CD-ROM.

Locating the Practice Files

After you have installed the practice files, all files that you need for this course will be stored in a folder named Word that is located on your hard disk. To navigate to this folder from within Word:

1　On the Standard toolbar, click the **Open** button.

2　Click the **Look In** down arrow and click the icon for your hard disk.

3　Double-click the folder named Word.

All the files for the lessons appear within this folder.

On the first page of each lesson, look for the margin icon *Practice files for this lesson.* This icon points to the paragraph that explains which file(s) you will need to work through the lesson exercises.

Microsoft Office Specialist Objectives

Each Microsoft Office Specialist certification level has a set of objectives, which are organised into broader skill sets. To prepare for the Microsoft Office Specialist certification exam, you should confirm that you can meet its objectives.

W2002-3-2

This book will prepare you fully for the Microsoft Office Specialist exam at the core level because it addresses all the objectives for this exam. Throughout this book, content that pertains to a Microsoft Office Specialist objective is identified with the Microsoft Office Specialist logo and objective number in the margin:

Core Microsoft Office Specialist Objectives

Objective	Skill
W2002-1	Inserting and Modifying Text
W2002-1-1	Insert, modify and move text and symbols
W2002-1-2	Apply and modify text formats
W2002-1-3	Correct spelling and grammar usage
W2002-1-4	Apply font and text effects
W2002-1-5	Enter and format date and time
W2002-1-6	Apply character styles
W2002-2	Creating and Modifying Paragraphs
W2002-2-1	Modify paragraph formats
W2002-2-2	Set and modify tabs
W2002-2-3	Apply bullet, outline and numbering format to paragraphs
W2002-2-4	Apply paragraph styles
W2002-3	Formatting Documents
W2002-3-1	Create and modify a header and footer
W2002-3-2	Apply and modify columns settings

Objective	Skill
W2002-3-3	Modify document layout and Page Setup options
W2002-3-4	Create and modify tables
W2002-3-5	Preview and print documents, envelopes and labels
W2002-4	Managing Documents
W2002-4-1	Manage files and folders for documents
W2002-4-2	Create documents using templates
W2002-4-3	Save documents using different names and file formats
W2002-5	Working with Graphics
W2002-5-1	Insert images and graphics
W2002-5-2	Create and modify diagrams and charts
W2002-6	Workgroup Collaboration
W2002-6-1	Compare and merge documents
W2002-6-2	Insert, view and edit comments
W2002-6-3	Convert documents into Web pages

Taking a Microsoft Office Specialist Exam

As desktop computing technology advances, more employers rely on the objectivity and consistency of technology certification when screening, hiring and training employees to ensure their competence. As an employee, you can use technology certification to prove that you meet the standards set by your current or potential employer. The Microsoft Office Specialist program is the only Microsoft-approved certification program designed to assist employees in validating their competence at using Microsoft Office applications.

About the Microsoft Office Specialist Program

A Microsoft Office Specialist is an individual who has certified his or her skills in one or more of the Microsoft Office desktop applications: Microsoft Word, Microsoft Excel, Microsoft PowerPoint, Microsoft Outlook, Microsoft Access, Microsoft FrontPage, or Microsoft Project. The Microsoft Office Specialist program typically offers certification exams at the "core" and "expert" skill levels. (The availability of Microsoft Office Specialist certification exams varies by application, application version and language. Visit *http;//www.microsoft.com/traincert/mcp/officespecialist* for exam availability.) The Microsoft Office Specialist Program is the only Microsoft-approved program in the world for certifying proficiency in Microsoft Office desktop applications and Microsoft Project. This certification can be a valuable asset when searching for a job or for career advancement.

If you want to take a Microsoft Office Specialist exam go to your nearest IQ CENTER® (IQ CENTER locations are listed at our Web site: www.certiport.com/IQCenters/IQCenterlocatorinternal.asp)

For Microsoft Office Specialist training courses go to you nearest Microsoft IT Academy Centre details of which can be found at the Microsoft web site.

A Microsoft IT Academy uses official Microsoft Office Approved Courseware and trains students to undertake the Microsoft Office Specialist exams, providing the end-user with a guaranteed high standard and quality of training. Courses are presented by Microsoft Certified Instructors, who are qualified in and have the know-how and experience to train students to this the industry gold standard for Office applications.

What Does This Logo Mean?

APPROVED COURSEWARE

It means this courseware has been approved by the Microsoft Office Specialist Program because it is the finest available for learning each Office XP application. It also means that upon completion of this courseware, you may be prepared to become a Microsoft Office Specialist.

Selecting a Microsoft Office Specialist Certification Level

In selecting the Microsoft Office Specialist certification levels that you would like to pursue, you should assess the following:

- The Office application and versions of the application with which you are familiar

- The length of time you have used the application

- Whether you have had formal or informal training

Candidates for the core-level Microsoft Office Specialist certification exams are expected to successfully complete a wide range of standard business tasks, such as formatting a document. Successful candidates generally have six or more months of experience with the application, including either formal instructor-led training with a Microsoft Office Specialist Authorized Instructor or self-study using Microsoft Office Specialist-approved books, guides, or interactive computer-based materials.

Candidates for expert-level certification, by comparison, are expected to complete more complex business-oriented assignments utilizing the application's advanced functionality, such as importing data and recording macros. Successful candidates generally have two or more years of experience with the application, again including formal instructor-led training with a Microsoft Office Specialist Authorized Instructor or self-study using Microsoft Office Specialist-approved materials.

Microsoft Office Specialist Exam Objectives

Every Microsoft Office Specialist certification exam is developed from a list of exam objectives, which are derived from studies of how the Office application is actually used in the workplace. Because these objectives dictate the scope of each exam, they provide you with critical information on how to prepare for Microsoft Office Specialist certification.

Microsoft Office Specialist Approved Courseware, including the Microsoft Press Step by Step series, is reviewed and approved on the basis of its coverage of the Microsoft Office Specialist exam objectives.

The Exam Experience

The Microsoft Office Specialist certification exams are unique in that they are performance-based examinations that allow you to interact with a "live" version of the Office application as you complete a series of assigned tasks. All the standard menus, toolbars and keyboard shortcuts are available—even the **Help** menu. Microsoft Office Specialist exams for Office XP applications consist of 25 to 35 questions, each of which requires you to complete one or more tasks using the Office application for which you are seeking certification. For example:

Prepare the document for publication as a Web page by completing the following three tasks:

1   Convert the memo to a Web page.

2   Title the page **Revised Company Policy**.

3   Name the memo **Policy Memo.htm**.

The duration of Microsoft Office Specialist exams ranges from 45 to 60 minutes, depending on the application. Passing percentages range from 70 to 80 percent correct.

The Exam Interface and Controls

After you fill out a series of information screens, the testing software starts the exam and the respective Office application. You will see the exam interface and controls, including the test question, in the dialog box in the lower right corner of the screen.

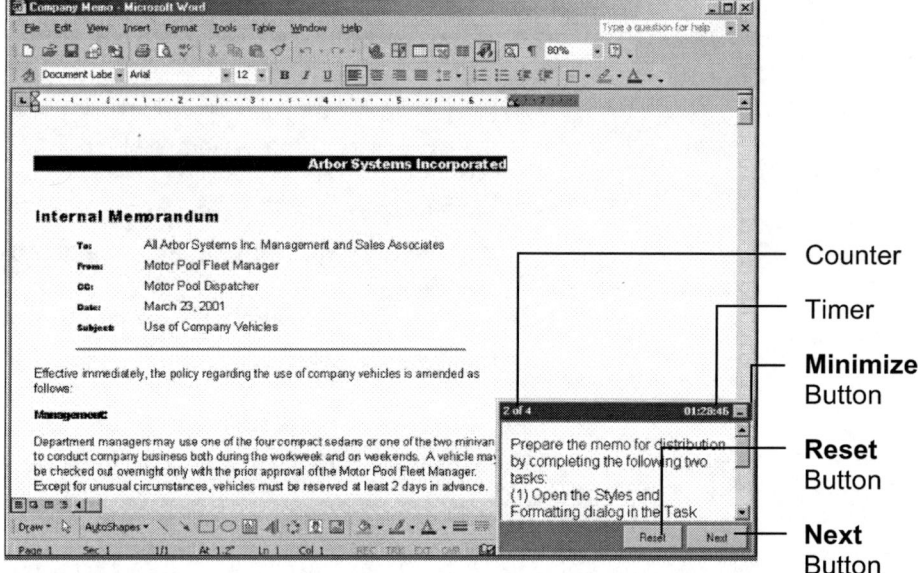

- If the exam dialog box gets in the way of your work, you can hide it by clicking the Minimize button in the upper right corner, or you can drag it to another position on the screen.

- The timer starts when the first question appears on your screen and displays the remaining exam time. The timer will not count the time required for the exam to be loaded between questions. It keeps track of only the time you spend answering questions. If the timer and the counter are distracting, click the timer to remove the display.

- The counter tracks how many questions you have completed and how many remain.

- The Reset button allows you to restart work on a question if you think you have made an error. The Reset button will not restart the entire exam or extend the exam time limit.

- When you complete a question, click the **Next** button to move to the next question.

important

It is not possible to move back to a previous question on the exam.

Test-Taking Tips

- Follow all instructions provided in each question completely and accurately.

- Enter requested information as it appears in the instructions but without duplicating the formatting. For example, all text and values that you will be asked to enter will appear in the instructions as bold and underlined; however, you should enter the information without applying this formatting unless you are specifically instructed to do otherwise.

- Close all dialog boxes before proceeding to the next exam question unless you are specifically instructed otherwise.

- There is no need to save your work before moving on to the next question unless you are specifically instructed otherwise.

- Do not cut and paste information from the exam interface into the application.

- For questions that ask you to print a document, spreadsheet, chart, report, slide and so forth, nothing will actually be printed.

- Responses are scored based on the result of your work, not the method you use to achieve that result (unless a specific method is explicitly required) and not the time you take to complete the question. Extra keystrokes or mouse clicks do not count against your score.

■ If your computer becomes unstable during the exam (for example, if the application's toolbars or the mouse no longer functions) or if a power outage occurs, contact a testing centre administrator immediately. The administrator will then restart the computer and the exam will return to the point before the interruption occurred.

Certification

At the conclusion of the exam, you will receive a score report, which you can print with the assistance of the testing centre administrator. If your score meets or exceeds the minimum required score, you will also be mailed a printed certificate within approximately 14 days.

For More Information

To learn more about becoming a Microsoft Office Specialist, visit *http;//www.microsoft.com/traincert/mcp/officespecialist.*

To purchase a Microsoft Office Specialist certification exam contact your nearest IQ testing centre.

Glossary

absolute The position of a picture that is determined by measurements you set.

attributes The characteristics that change the appearance of text. You can change the appearance of text by making it bold, italic, or coloured.

AutoCorrect A feature that corrects commonly misspelled words as you type.

bookmark A location in a document that is used to mark text so that you or your reader can return to it quickly.

bullet A small graphic, such as a large dot, that sets off an item in a list.

cell The intersection of a row and a column in a datasheet.

character style A style for selected words and lines of text within a paragraph.

charts Graphics that use lines, bars, columns, pie slices, or other markers to represent numbers and other values.

check box form field A form field that lets you provide several options so that users can click one or more to indicate their choices.

column headings Gray buttons across the top of a datasheet.

comments Electronic notes about text or other parts of a document.

cross-reference An entry that refers the reader to another entry.

data marker A graphical element, such as a bar or area, in a chart that represents a value in a datasheet.

data series A group of related data points in a datasheet.

datasheet A numerical representation of data in cells that form rows and columns.

data source A document that is combined with the main document in the mail merge process.

data table A grid attached to a chart that shows the data used to create the chart.

desktop publishing A process that combines text and graphics in an appealing and easy to read format, such as a report, newsletter, or book.

destination file The file into which you are inserting information.

diagram A visual and relational representation of information, such as an organization chart.

digital signature A secure electronic stamp of authentication on a document.

docked toolbar A toolbar that is attached to the edge of the Word window.

drawing canvas An area that contains drawing shapes and pictures.

drop-down form field A form field that lets you provide predefined answers so that users are limited to specified choices.

embedded object An object that becomes part of the destination file and is no longer a part of the source file.

endnotes References or citations that appear at the end of a document.

entry An index listing.

file Information, such as a document, that a program saves with a unique name.

file format The way that a program stores a file so that the program can open it.

fill effect The pattern, colour, or texture in a chart element.

filter To exclude records from a data list in a mail merge.

filtered Web page An optimized Web page.

floating toolbar A toolbar that is not attached to an edge of the Word window.

font See font typeface.

font effects A way to emphasize text using formatting options, such as bold type, italics, all capital letters, or shadows.

font size The size of text, usually expressed in points.

font typeface A complete set of characters that uses the same design.

footer The text that is printed at the bottom of each page.

footnotes References or citations that appear at the end of each page.

form field properties Settings that allow you to change form field attributes, such as text field length or the check box default setting.

form fields Predefined places where users enter their answers to the questions on a form.

forms Printed or online documents with instructions, questions and fields (blanks) where users can enter their responses.

formula A mathematical expression that performs calculations, such as adding or averaging values.

frame A window region on a Web page.

graphic A picture or a drawing object.

gridlines Lines that appear in a chart to make it easier to view the data.

header The text that is printed at the top of each page.

HTML See Hypertext Markup Language.

hyperlinks Links to a location in the same file, another file, or an HTML page that are represented by coloured and underlined text or by a graphic.

Hypertext Markup Language (HTML) The markup language of tags that creates Web pages.

indent markers Markers along the ruler that you use to control how text wraps on the left or right side of a document.

indented index An index that uses subentries on separate lines below the main entries.

index A list of the topics, names and terms used in a document along with the corresponding page numbers, which typically appears at the end of a document.

key combination Two or more keys pressed at the same time that perform an action.

landscape Horizontal orientation in which the page is wider than it is tall.

legend A chart element that identifies the patterns or colours assigned to the data.

link bar A collection of graphic or text buttons representing hyperlinks to pages in a Web site and external Web sites.

linked object An object that maintains a direct link to the source file.

links See hyperlinks.

macro A recorded series of commands (keystrokes and instructions) that are treated as a single command.

mail merge The process of combining a data source document and a main document to create a single merged document.

main document The document that is combined with the data source in the mail merge process.

manual page break A page break that you insert in a document. A manual page break appears as a dotted line across the page with the label *Page Break*.

master document A document that contains a set of subdocuments.

merge The process of combining a data source document and a main document to create a single merged document.

merge fields Placeholders that indicate where Word inserts personalized information from a data source.

module A location within a Visual Basic project where a macro is stored.

Normal view The default editing view, which you use to write and edit documents.

note separator The line that divides the notes from the body of the document.

note text The content of the footnote or endnote.

Object Linking and Embedding (OLE) A feature that allows you to insert a file created in one program into a document that was created in another program.

Office Assistant A help system that answers questions, offers tips and provides help for Microsoft Office XP program features.

Office Clipboard A storage area shared by all Office programs where multiple pieces of information from several different sources are stored.

orphan The first line of a paragraph printed by itself at the bottom of a page.

Outline view A view that shows the structure of a document, which consists of headings and body text.

page orientation The way in which a page is laid out in a printed document.

paragraph Any amount of text that ends when you press the ⏎ Enter key.

paragraph styles Styles for entire paragraphs, including their indents, alignment and tabs.

Personalized menus Menus that adjust so that only the commands that you use most often appear on the short menus.

picture A photograph, a scanned picture, a bitmap, or clip art that was created outside of Word.

plot area The area that includes the data markers and the category (x) and value (y) axes in a chart.

point A measurement for the size of text. A point is equal to about 1/72 of an inch.

portrait Vertical orientation in which the page is taller than it is wide.

Print Layout view A view that shows a document as it appears on the printed page.

project An executable program that is stored in a Word document or template.

publishing The process of saving a file as a Web page or Web site on a Web server for viewing on the World Wide Web or on a network.

query A set of selection criteria that indicate how to filter recipients in a mail merge.

read-only A setting that lets a user read or copy the file, but not change or save it.

record A single set of items in a data source.

reference mark A number or character in the main text of a document that indicates additional information is included in a footnote or endnote.

relative The position of a picture that is determined by its relation to other specified parts of the document, such as the margin, the page, a column, or a character.

Reviewing Pane A pane that shows information related to the changes and comments in a document.

Reviewing toolbar A toolbar that contains buttons that let you accept and reject changes and comments.

row headings Gray buttons along the left side of a datasheet.

run-in index An index that lists subentries on the same line as the main entries in an index.

section break A portion of a document that you can format with unique page settings, such as different margins. A section break appears as a double-dotted line across the page with the words *Section Break* and the type of section break in the middle.

selection area A blank area to the left of a document's left margin that you can click to select parts of the document.

Smart Tag A button that helps you control the result of certain actions, such as automatic text correction, automatic layout behaviour, or copy and paste.

soft page break A page break that Word inserts in a document. A soft page break appears as a dotted line across the page.

sort To arrange information in a logical order.

source file The original document created in the source program.

source program The program that created a document that is a linked object in Word.

spelling and grammar A feature that corrects errors and maintains professional writing standards.

style A collection of text and paragraph formatting choices that you can apply to text throughout a document.

Style area An area along the left side of a document that displays style names.

subdocuments Sets of related documents that are used in master documents.

subentry A subtopic index listing.

tab leader An index format that separates the entry from the page number associated with it. Tab leaders can be dotted, dashed, or solid lines.

tab stop A location along the ruler that you use to align text.

Table AutoFormat A set of 18 predesigned table formats that include a variety of borders, colours and attributes that will give a table a professional look.

table of contents A list of the main headings and subheadings in a document along with corresponding page numbers, which typically appears at the beginning of a document.

task pane A pane that allows you to access commands related to a specific task quickly without having to use menus and toolbars.

template A special document that stores text, styles, formatting, macros and page information for use in other documents.

text form field A form field that lets you provide several types of text boxes so that users can enter text.

theme A unified look in a document that incorporates heading and text styles.

thesaurus A feature that looks up alternative words or synonyms for a word.

Uniform Resource Locator (URL) A unique address for a page on the Web, such as *http://www.microsoft.com.*

version A record of changes made to a document.

watermarks Dimmed pictures or text that appears faintly in the background of a printed document.

Web archive A Web site that saves all the elements, including text and graphics, into a single document.

Web Layout view A view that shows a document as it appears as a Web page.

Web page A special document in HTML designed to be viewed in a Web browser.

Web server A storage location where you save a Web site or Web page for viewing on the World Wide Web or on a network.

Web site A collection of Web pages with navigation tools and a designed theme.

widow The last line of a paragraph printed by itself at the top of a page.

WordArt A feature that allows you to change the shape and appearance of text in a document.

word processing A process by which you create, edit and produce text documents.

word wrap The movement of text to the next line when typing goes beyond the right margin.

workgroup templates Templates shared over a network.

XE An index entry field code that defines the text and page number for an index entry and other options, such as a subentry text.

LESSON 1

Creating a Document

After completing this lesson, you will be able to:

✓ *Get started with Word.*

✓ *Create a document.*

✓ *Work with an existing document*

✓ *Edit a document.*

✓ *Replace text in a document.*

Word processing is using a computer program to create, edit and produce text documents. Word-processing programs help you create professional-quality documents because they let you type and format text, correct errors and preview your work before you print or distribute a document.

Microsoft Word is a word-processing program that you can use to compose and update a wide range of business and personal documents. In addition, Word offers many **desktop-publishing** features that let you enhance the appearance of documents so that they are appealing and easy to read. Whether you need to create a letter, memo, fax, annual report, newsletter, or book, Word has the power and flexibility to produce professional documents quickly and easily.

In this lesson, you'll create and edit documents for The Garden Company, a business that provides supplies to gardeners. You'll start by entering text to create a document and then you'll save the document as a file. You'll open other documents to navigate and switch between them. As you save a document with a new file name, you'll also create a folder for the file. Finally, you'll edit a document by inserting and deleting text, moving and copying text and finding and replacing text.

This lesson uses the practice files ExistDoc, EditDoc, OpenDoc and ReplaceText that you installed from this book's CD-ROM. For details about installing the practice files, see "Using the Book's CD-ROM" at the beginning of this book.

important

If you haven't done so yet, you should install the book's practice files so that you can work through the exercises in this lesson. You can find instructions for installing the practice files in the "Using the Book's CD-ROM" section at the beginning of the book.

Getting Started with Word

When you start Word, the Word program window opens. This window contains many of the same menus, tools and other features that every Microsoft Office XP program has and some that are unique to Word. You enter and edit text in the Word document window, which is part of the Word program window. The insertion point, the blinking vertical line that appears in the document window, indicates where the text will appear when you type.

The toolbars contain groups of buttons which provide quick access to the most frequently used functions.

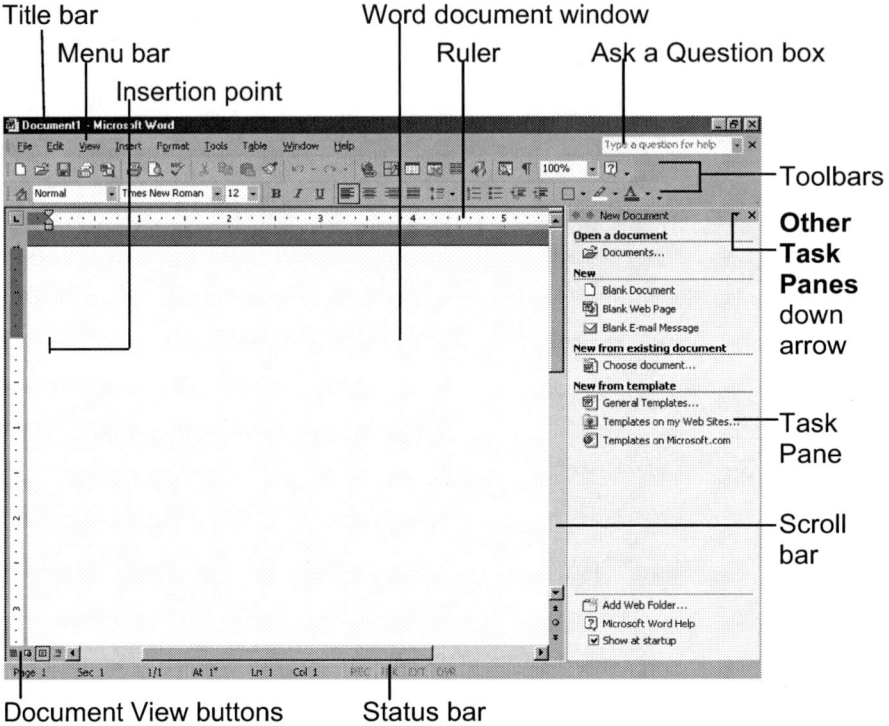

Title bar
Menu bar
Insertion point
Word document window
Ruler
Ask a Question box
Toolbars
Other Task Panes down arrow
Task Pane
Scroll bar
Document View buttons
Status bar

tip

Word uses personalized menus and toolbars to reduce the number of menu commands and toolbar buttons that you see on the screen and to display the ones that you use most often. When you click a menu name, a short menu appears, containing the commands that you use most often. To make the complete long menu appear, you can leave the pointer over the menu name for several seconds, double-click the menu name, or click the menu name and then click the small double arrow at the bottom of the short menu. When the long menu is open, the commands that did not appear on the short menu are light grey.

important

The default setting for the Standard and Formatting toolbars is for them to share one row, which prevents you from seeing all the buttons. The **Toolbar Options** down arrow at the end of the toolbar gives you access to the other buttons. If a button mentioned in this book doesn't appear on a toolbar, click the **Toolbar Options** down arrow on that toolbar to display the rest of its buttons. To make it easier for you to find buttons, the Standard and Formatting toolbars in this book appear on two rows. To change your settings to match the screens in this book, click **Customize** on the **Tools** menu, select the **Show Standard and Formatting toolbars on two rows** check box on the **Options** tab and then click **Close**.

At the bottom of the document window are view buttons that allow you to look at a document in different ways. **Normal view** is the default editing view, which you use to write and edit your documents. **Web Layout view** shows your document as it appears as a Web page. This view is useful for viewing and editing text and graphics designed for use in a Web browser. **Print Layout view** shows your document as it appears on the printed page. This view is useful for changing page and column boundaries, editing headers and footers and working with drawing objects. **Outline view** shows the structure of the document, which consists of headings and body text. This view is useful for viewing, moving, copying and reorganizing text.

Task pane
new for
OfficeXP

Word organizes commands for common tasks in the **task pane**, a small window next to your document that opens when you need it. For example, when you start Word, you see the **New Document** task pane, which includes commands for opening and creating documents. Use the **New Document** task pane to open a saved or blank document, to create a document based on an existing one, or to create a document from a **template**, a file containing structure and style settings that help you create a specific type of document, such as a memo or resumé. You also can show or hide any task pane when you like. If you want to use a task pane and the one that you want does not appear, you can manually show the task pane and then select the specific task pane that you want from the **Other Task Panes** menu on the task pane. If you no longer need the task pane, you can hide it to free up valuable screen space in the program window. On the **View** menu, click **Task Pane**; clicking the command hides the task pane if it is currently displayed or shows it if it is currently hidden.

tip

The task pane opens each time you start Word and closes when you open a document. If you do not want the task pane to appear each time you start Word, clear the **Show at Startup** check box in the task pane.

Ask A Question box
new for
OfficeXP

When you have a question about using Word, you can save time by using the Ask A Question box rather than searching the table of contents or index in online Help. After you type a question or keyword and press the ⟨ Enter ⟩ key, Word lists Help topics so that you can choose the one that answers your question. Another way to get help is to use the **Office Assistant**. The Office Assistant offers tips for completing your task, such as creating and formatting a letter. For complete access to Help topics, you can open the Help window and use its table of contents, index and Answer Wizard, or you can visit the Microsoft Web site to find Help information.

In this exercise, you start Word, close the **New Document** task pane and ask a question about online Help.

1   On the taskbar, click **Start**, point to **Programs** and then click **Microsoft Word**.

     The Word window opens with a blank document and the **New Document** task pane in the document window.

tip

Another way to start Word and create a new document is to click the **New Office Document** command at the top of the **Start** menu. When the **New Office Document** dialog box appears, double-click the **Blank Document** icon.

2 In the title bar of the **New Document** task pane, click the **Other Task Panes** down arrow.

The **Other Task Panes** menu opens.

3 Press the Esc key, or click an empty place in the document.

Word closes the **Other Task Panes** menu.

Close

4 Click the **Close** button in the **New Document** task pane.

The **New Document** task pane closes.

5 On the **View** menu, click **Task Pane**.

The **New Document** task pane opens.

6 On the right side of the menu bar, click in the **Ask A Question** box.

7 Type How do you use help? and then press Enter.

A menu appears with Help topics that relate to the question that you typed.

8 Click **About getting help while you work**.

The Microsoft Word Help window opens.

9 Click the topic **Ask a Question box**.

The Microsoft Word Help window displays more information about the Ask A Question box.

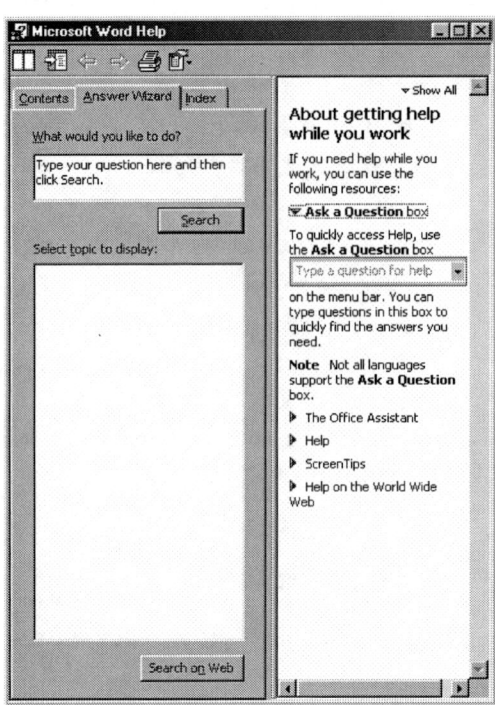

Close

10 Click the **Close** button to close the Microsoft Word Help window.

11 On the **Help** menu, click **Show the Office Assistant**.

The animated paper clip Office Assistant appears.

12 Click the **Office Assistant**.

A yellow help box appears, as shown in the following illustration:

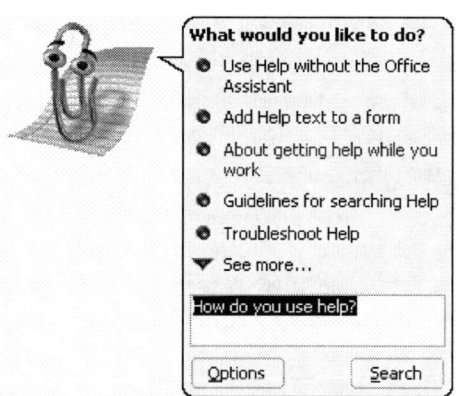

You can type a question in the box and then click **Search** or click a Help topic provided.

You can hide the Office Assistant permanently by deactivating the **Use the Office Assistant** option on the **Options** tab of the **Office Assistant** dialog box.

13 Right-click the Office Assistant and then click **Hide** on the shortcut menu to hide the Office Assistant.

tip

To turn off the Office Assistant and use the Microsoft Help window or the Ask A Question box, right-click the **Office Assistant**, click **Options**, clear the **Use the Office Assistant** check box and then click **OK**. On the **Help** menu, click **Microsoft Word Help**. To turn on the Office Assistant again, click **Show the Office Assistant** on the **Help** menu.

Creating a Document

W2002-1-1
W2002-4-1
W2002-4-3

Creating a Word document is as simple as typing text. The insertion point indicates where the text will appear in the document. When the text you're typing goes beyond the right margin, Word "wraps" the text to the next line. **Word wrap,** a common feature of word processing and desktop publishing programs, means that pressing [Enter] starts a new paragraph, not a new line.

The text that you type appears in the document window and is stored by the computer, but only temporarily. If you want to keep a copy of the text, you must save the document to a **file**. You specify a name and location for the file. You can then retrieve the file later to continue working on the document.

Create New Folder

To save a new document in Word, you click the **Save** button on the Standard toolbar. The first time that you save a document, you use the **Save As** dialog box to enter a file name and indicate where you want to save the file. To keep your documents organised and easily accessible, you can store them in folders that you create. You can store related documents in a single folder. To create a new folder, you click the **Create New Folder** button in the **Save As** dialog box.

Save

After you save a document once using the **Save As** dialog box, you can save changes that you make by clicking the **Save** button on the Standard toolbar. In other words, the newer version overwrites the original version. If you want to keep both the original file and the version with your recent changes, you click the **Save As** command on the **File** menu to save the new version with a new name. You can save the document with the new name in the same folder as the original or in a new folder, but you cannot store two documents in the same folder if the documents have the same name.

The Garden Company is preparing a new garden supply catalogue. The inside cover of the catalogue will need some text that describes the new catalogue's theme, which is planning a garden.

In this exercise, you enter text in a document and then save your new document.

New Blank Document

1   On the Standard toolbar, click the **New Blank Document** button.

A new document window opens.

2   With the insertion point at the top of the new document, type **Gardeners, Get Your Garden Tools Ready!** and then press Enter .

The text appears in the new document.

3   Press Enter again to insert a blank line below the heading.

4   Type **With spring just around the corner, let's start thinking flowers and vegetables. Let's start planning for this year's garden. Let's start celebrating blue-ribbon zinnias and zucchini. Let's get your garden tools ready.**

Notice that you did not need to press Enter when the insertion point reached the right margin because the text wrapped to the left margin.

important

If a wavy red or green line appears under a word or phrase, Word is flagging text that it does not recognize as a possible spelling or grammar error. If a wavy blue line appears under a word or phrase, Word is detecting inconsistent formatting. If a purple dotted line appears under a word or phrase, Word is displaying a Smart Tag, which recognizes certain types of text as data that you can use with other programs. For example, Word tags a person's name as data that you can add to an electronic address book. For now, ignore any errors and Smart Tags.

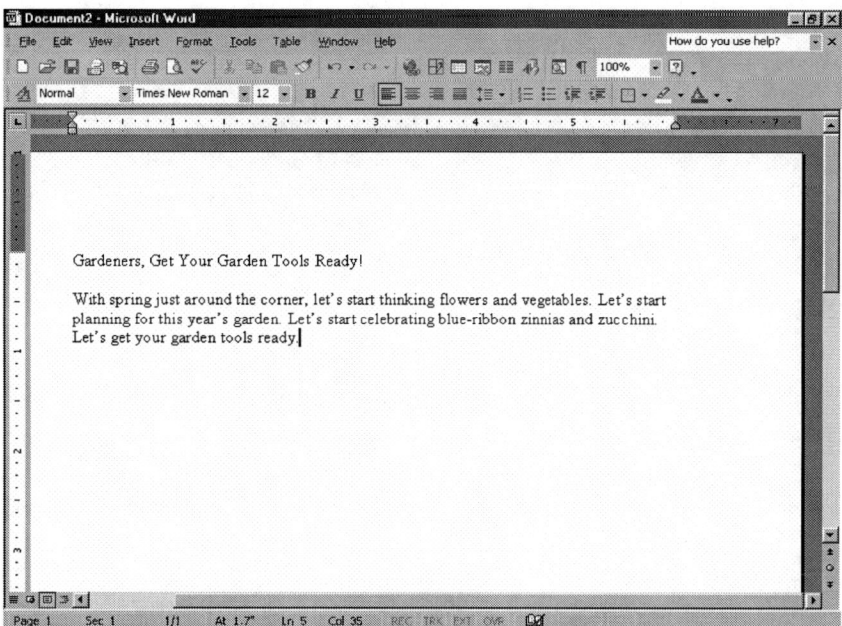

Save

5 On the Standard toolbar, click the **Save** button.

The **Save As** dialog box appears and displays the My Documents folder as the open folder.

tip

To help you locate the drive where you want to store a new folder and file, you can click the **Up One Level** button to move up a level in the hierarchy of folders, or you can use the Places Bar to move to another location on your computer. The **Places Bar** on the left side of the **Save As** and **Open** dialog boxes provides quick access to commonly used locations for storing and opening files. For instance, to save a file to a floppy disk, you click the **Desktop** icon on the **Places Bar**, double- click the **My Computer** icon and then double-click **3 Floppy (A:)**.

6 Click the **Save in** down arrow and then click your hard disk, typically drive C.

7 In the list of file and folder names, double-click the **SBS** folder and then double-click the **Word** folder.

The contents of the Word folder appear in the **Save As** dialog box.

8 Double-click the **CreatingDoc** folder.

The contents of the CreatingDoc folder appear in the **Save As** dialog box. You can see that the word *Gardeners*, the first word in the document, appears in the **File name** box.

tip

Word uses the first few characters (or words) in the document to suggest a file name. You can accept this suggested name or type a new one. Depending on your Windows setup, file names might appear with an extension, which is a dot followed by a three-letter program identifier. For Word, the extension is .doc.

Create New Folder

9 Click the **Create New Folder** button.

The **New Folder** dialog box appears. The folder that you are creating is a subfolder within the CreatingDoc folder.

10 Type **NewFolder** and then click **OK**.

NewFolder becomes the current folder.

11 In the **File name** box, double-click **Gardeners**, type **FirstSave** and then click the **Save** button.

The **Save As** dialog box closes and the file name *FirstSave* appears in the title bar.

Document Recovery task pane
new for
OfficeXP

important

Word saves documents for recovery in case the program stops responding or you lose power. The **Document Recovery** task pane lists all recovered documents and allows you to open the documents, view the repairs and compare the recovered versions. Word saves the changes in a recovery file based on the amount of time indicated in the AutoRecover option. To turn on the AutoRecover option and specify a time interval in which to save, on the **Tools** menu, click **Options**, click the **Save** tab, select the **Save AutoRecover info every** check box, specify the period of time and then click **OK**.

Close Window

12 Click the **Close Window** button in the document window.

The FirstSave document closes.

Saving a File for Use in Another Program

W2002-4-3

Word allows you to save a document in a file format other than the Word document format. A **file format** is the way that a program stores a file so that the program can open up the file later. Saving a document in another format is important if you share documents with others who use programs or previous versions of Word that have a different file format, such as Word 6.0/95 or WordPerfect. For example, if you use Word 6.0 on the computer that you have at home, you can create a document in Word 2002, save it in the Word 6.0 format and then open and edit the document on your home computer.

Show Document
Format
new for
OfficeXP

If you are not sure of the version of a document, you can use the **Properties** dialog box to display file format information about the document, which includes the version, type and creator of the file. On the **File** menu, click **Properties** and then click the **General** tab to display the document format information.

To save a file in another file format:

1   On the **File** menu, click **Save As**.

     The **Save As** dialog box appears.

2   In the **File name** box, type a new name for the document.

3   Click the **Save as type** down arrow and then select the file format that you want to use.

4   Click **Save**.

Working with an Existing Document

Once you save a document to a file, you can open that document again. To open an existing document, you use the **Open** button on the Standard toolbar or an option on the **New Document** task pane. Using the **New Document** task pane, you can create a document based on an existing one. This is useful when you want to start a new document with existing text without changing the original document.

To enter or revise text, you start by positioning the insertion point. You can click to place the insertion point at a particular location, or you can press keys on the keyboard to move the insertion point in a document. When you use a **key combination**, you press two keys at the same time to perform an action. For example, pressing the ⌐End⌐ key moves the insertion point to the end of a line of text, whereas pressing the ⌐Ctrl⌐ and ⌐End⌐ keys at the same time moves the insertion point to the beginning of the document. To use a key combination, you hold down the first key (for example, ⌐Ctrl⌐) and then press the second key (for example, ⌐End⌐). Once the action takes place, you release both keys.

The following table shows the keys and key combinations that you can use to move the insertion point quickly.

Pressing this key	Moves the insertion point
←	Left one character at a time
→	Right one character at a time
↓	Down one line at a time
↑	Up one line at a time
Ctrl + ←	Left one word at a time
Ctrl + →	Right one word at a time
Home	To the beginning of the current line of text
End	To the end of the current line of text
Ctrl + Home	To the start of the document
Ctrl + End	To the end of the document
Ctrl + Page Up	To the beginning of the previous page
Ctrl + Page Down	To the beginning of the next page
Page Up	Up one screen
Page Down	Down one screen

You can also use the vertical and horizontal scroll bars to move around in a document. However, using the scroll bars does not move the insertion point—it changes only your view of the document in the window. For example, if you drag the vertical scroll box down to the bottom of the scroll bar, the end of the document comes into view, but the insertion point does not move. The status bar shows the location of the insertion point (by page, section, inch, line and column). Click the **up** or **down** scroll arrow on the vertical scroll bar to move the document window up or down one line of text. Click the left or right scroll arrow on the horizontal scroll bar to move the document window to the left or right several characters at a time.

Select Browse Object

As you create longer documents, you can use the **Select Browse Object** menu at the bottom of the vertical scroll bar to move quickly through a document. When you click the **Select Browse Object** button, a menu appears with browsing options, such as **Browse by Page**, **Browse by Comment** and **Browse by Graphic**.

When you open a document, a program button with the Word program icon and document name appears on the taskbar. You can have many documents open at the same time, but only one is the current or active document. The program button of the current document appears pressed in. To move between open documents, click the program button on the taskbar, or use the **Window** menu, which lists all open documents. The check mark to the left of the document name in the **Window** menu indicates the current document.

The Garden Company sends marketing letters to its customers during the spring to promote new products. Before the letter is updated, the copy editor wants to review last year's letter to see what needs to be changed.

ExistDoc OpenDoc

Open

In this exercise, you move around a document and then switch between open documents. First, you open the document called ExistDoc and then you move around the document to review the text.

1   On the Standard toolbar, click the **Open** button.

     The **Open** dialog box appears.

2   Navigate to the **SBS** folder on your hard disk, double-click the **Word** folder and then double-click the **CreatingDoc** folder.

3   Double-click the **ExistDoc** file to open the document in the Word window.

     The ExistDoc document opens.

tip

If a document doesn't open when you try to open it through the **Open** dialog box, you can repair it. On the Standard toolbar, click the **Open** button, select the file you want to open, click the **Open down arrow** and then click **Open and Repair**.

4   In the greeting, click after the colon (:) to position the insertion point.

5 Press the `Home` key to move the insertion point to the beginning of the line.

6 Press the `→` key five times to move the insertion point to the beginning of the word *Garden* in the greeting.

7 Press `↓` two times to move the insertion point to the first paragraph.

8 Press the `End` key to move the insertion point to the end of the line of text.

9 Press `Ctrl` + `End` to move the insertion point to the end of the document.

10 Press `Ctrl` + `Home` to move the insertion point to the beginning of the document.

11 Drag the vertical scroll box to the bottom of the vertical scroll bar.

The insertion point is still at the beginning of the document, but the end of the document now comes into view.

12 In the vertical scroll bar, click the scroll up arrow five times.

The document changes to show five more lines of text.

13 Click above the vertical scroll box to change the view of the document by one screen.

14 In the horizontal scroll bar, click the right scroll arrow twice so that the right side of the document comes into view by a few characters.

15 Drag the horizontal scroll box all the way to the left.

The document is repositioned. Note that the location of the insertion point has not changed—just the view of the document.

16 Press `Ctrl` + `Home` to move the insertion point to the beginning of the document.

Select Browse Object

17 Click the **Select Browse Object** button on the right side of the window.

When you click the button, a palette of objects appears.

18 Move the pointer over the palette of objects.

The name of each object in the palette appears as you point to an object.

Browse by Page

19 Click the **Browse by Page** button.

The insertion point moves from page 1 to the beginning of page 2.

20 On the Standard toolbar, click the **Open** button.

The **Open** dialog box appears.

21 Navigate to the **SBS** folder on your hard disk, double-click the **Word** folder, double-click the **CreatingDoc** folder and then double-click the **OpenDoc** file.

The OpenDoc document opens.

22 On the taskbar, click the **ExistDoc** program button to make it the current document.

The ExistDoc document becomes the top window. The taskbar shows two program buttons, each with the name of an open document. The button that is pressed in indicates the active document, which is currently the ExistDoc document.

tip
You can set Word to show only one program button. On the **Tools** menu, click **Options**, click the **View** tab, clear the **Windows in Taskbar** and then click **OK**.

23 On the menu bar, click **Window**.

The two open files are listed at the bottom of the **Window** menu.

24 On the **Window** menu, click **Arrange All**.

The two document windows are resized and stacked one on top of the other.

Close Window

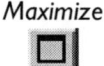

25 Click the **Close Window** button in the ExistDoc document window and then click the **Close Window** button in the OpenDoc document window.

Maximize

26 Click the **Maximize** button in the Word window to return the Word window to its original size.

Editing a Document

W2002-1-1

Editing a document also means overtyping existing text.

When you edit a document, you revise its text. Editing encompasses many tasks, such as inserting and deleting words and phrases, correcting errors and moving and copying text to different places in the document. Editing also includes searching for words, phrases, or even formatting and replacing that text with different text.

Inserting text is as easy as positioning the insertion point and typing. When you insert text, existing text moves to the right to accommodate the text that you are inserting and the text that reaches the right margin wraps to the next line, if necessary.

Before you can edit or work with text, you first need to select it. Selected text appears highlighted on the screen. To select a block of text quickly, you can use the selection area. The **selection area** is a blank area to the left of the document's left margin. When the pointer is in the selection area, it changes from an I-beam to a right-pointing arrow. To deselect text, click anywhere outside the selected text.

Selection area

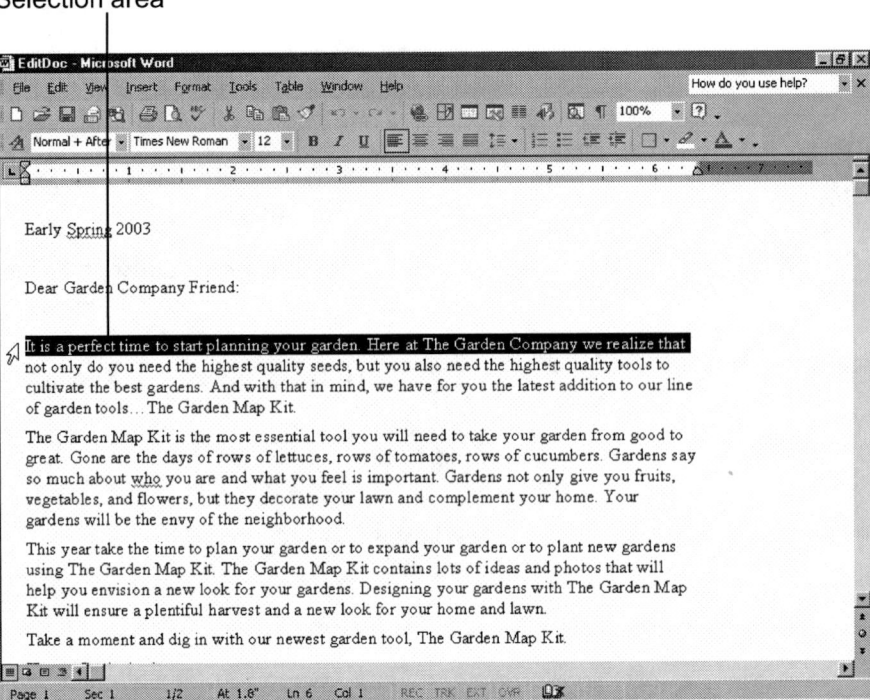

Select nonadjacent text
new for OfficeXP

To select blocks of text that are not adjacent in a document, you select the first block of text, hold down Ctrl and then select the next block of text. You can also use the Shift key and the arrow keys to select adjacent words, lines, or paragraphs. You position the insertion point in the text that you want to select, hold down the Shift key and then press an arrow key or click at the end of the text that you want to select.

The following table describes methods that you can use to select text in a document.

Selection	Action
A word	Double-click the word.
A line	Click the selection area to the left of the line.
A sentence	Click anywhere in the sentence while holding down the Ctrl key. The sentence is selected from the first character up to and including any spacing following the last punctuation mark.
A paragraph	Double-click the selection area to the left of the paragraph, or triple-click anywhere in the paragraph.
An entire document	Click anywhere in the selection area while holding down the Ctrl key, or triple-click in the selection area.

Deleting text in a document is also an easy task. To delete a few characters, you can use the [Backspace] or [Del] key. Pressing [Backspace] deletes the character to the left of the insertion point. Pressing [Del] deletes the character to the right of the insertion point. Using these keys is a quick way to correct small errors. However, if you need to delete an entire sentence or a large block of text, first select the text and then press [Backspace] or [Del].

Undo

As you edit a document, Word keeps track of the changes that you make so that you can easily remove a change and restore your original text. This is useful when you make a mistake, as when you inadvertently delete a word. To undo the last action that you performed, click the **Undo** button on the Standard toolbar. To display the last five or six actions that you have performed, click the down arrow on the **Undo** button. Click the action in the list that you want to undo and that action and all subsequent actions in the list are undone.

Redo

If you undo an action, you can restore, or redo, the action by clicking the **Redo** button. You can click the down arrow on the **Redo** button to restore multiple undone actions.

Office Clipboard
new for
OfficeXP

You can move selected text by cutting it and then pasting it in another place in the document. Text that you move, or cut, no longer appears in the document but is temporarily stored in an area of the computer memory called the **Office Clipboard**. Copying text is similar to moving text. However, when you copy selected text, the selected text remains in its original location and you paste a copy of the selected text in another location. When you paste the selection, the text appears at the location of the insertion point.

Clipboard Icon

You can use the Office Clipboard to store multiple items of information from several different sources in one storage area shared by all Office programs. The Office Clipboard appears as a task pane and shows all the items that you stored there. You can paste these items of information into any Office program, either individually or all at once.

The Office Clipboard appears when you copy multiple items, unless the Office Clipboard option is turned off. To manually open the Office Clipboard, you click **Office Clipboard** on the **Edit** menu or double-click the **Clipboard** icon in the status area of the taskbar. The Clipboard icon appears on the taskbar when the Office Clipboard contains items. The Office Clipboard is useful for moving and copying information between pages and documents. If you need to move or copy text within a paragraph or line, you can drag the text instead of using the Office Clipboard. To move text, you select the text and drag it to another place. To copy or select text, you hold down [Ctrl] and drag it to another place.

Multiuser editing
new for
OfficeXP

If you work on a network, more than one person at a time can edit the same document. When you open a document that is already open, choose to create a local copy and merge your changes later. When you finish editing and close the document, other users who have the document open can see your changes and merge them into the document.

Now that the marketing letter from last year has been reviewed, an assistant at The Garden Company can use it to create a new letter for this year's marketing campaign. The most efficient way to create the new letter is to edit last year's letter.

EditDoc

In this exercise, you edit text in the existing document. You insert and delete text, undo the deletion, copy and paste a phrase and move a paragraph.

Open

1   On the Standard toolbar, click the **Open** button.

The **Open** dialog box appears.

2   Navigate to the **SBS** folder on your hard disk, double-click the **Word** folder, double- click the **CreatingDoc** folder and then double-click the **EditDoc** file.

The EditDoc document opens.

3   Double-click the word *Early* at the top of the document to select it and then press [Enter] to delete the word and create a paragraph.

4   Press [End] to move the insertion point to the end of the line, press [Space] and then type **Has Arrived!**

The text appears at the end of the line.

5   Press [↓] four times, hold down [Ctrl] and then click anywhere in the sentence to select it.

6   Press [Del] to delete the sentence.

Undo

7   On the Standard toolbar, click the **Undo** button to restore the deleted text.

8   Click the down scroll arrow until the phrase *Happy Gardening!* appears, position the mouse pointer in the selection area to the left of the text *Happy Gardening!* and then click to select the entire line of text.

Copy

9   On the Standard toolbar, click the **Copy** button to copy the text to the Clipboard.

10   On the **Edit** menu, click **Office Clipboard**.

The **Clipboard** task pane appears, displaying the current items in the Office Clipboard.

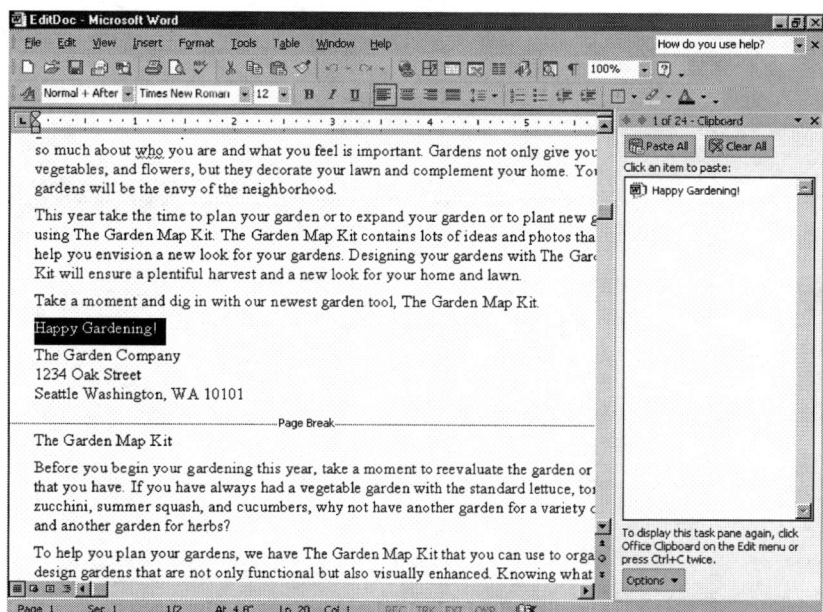

troubleshooting

You can turn on and off Office Clipboard options in the task pane. You can choose either to display the Office Clipboard when you are copying items or to copy items to the Office Clipboard without displaying the Office Clipboard. You can also choose to display the Clipboard icon on the taskbar when the Office Clipboard is turned on. To access these options, click Options at the bottom of the Clipboard task pane.

11 Press ⌈Ctrl⌋ **+** ⌈End⌋ to move the insertion point to the end of the document and then press ⌈Enter⌋ to insert a blank line.

troubleshooting

If a Paste Options button appears next to the selection that you pasted, you can ignore it for now. The Paste Options button provides a list of options that allows you to determine how the information is pasted into your document.

12 In the **Clipboard** task pane, click the *Happy Gardening!* box to place the text from the Clipboard into the document.

Close

13 In the **Clipboard** task pane, click the **Close** button to close the task pane.

14 If necessary, scroll up to the paragraph that begins *The Garden Company welcomes your comments* and then triple-click in the paragraph to select the paragraph.

15 Drag the paragraph text down to above the text *Happy Gardening!*.

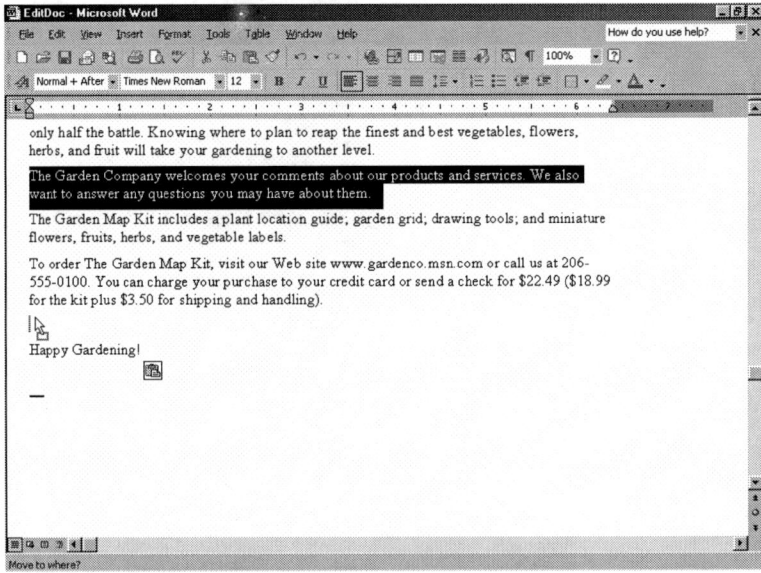

When you release the mouse, the text appears in its new location.

16   On the Standard toolbar, click the **Save** button to save the document.

17   Click the **Close Window** button in the document window.

The EditDoc document closes.

Close

Replacing Text in a Document

W2002-1-1

Word corrects commonly misspelled words as you type so that you don't have to correct them yourself. For example, if you type *teh*, Word changes it to *the* as soon as you press ⟨ Space ⟩. Changing the text like this is called **AutoCorrect**. Besides correcting misspelled words, AutoCorrect can also insert a long phrase when you type an abbreviation. For example, if you type the abbreviation *gc* to represent the company name, you can have AutoCorrect insert the full phrase *The Garden Company*. To add your own AutoCorrect entry, you enter the abbreviation and the full phrase in the **AutoCorrect** dialog box and then add the entry to the list of corrections.

AutoCorrect Options

If you don't want Word to automatically change text, you can undo the change or turn off AutoCorrect options by clicking the **AutoCorrect Options** button that appears after the change. The **AutoCorrect Options** button first appears as a small blue box near the changed text and then changes to a button icon. If you are uncertain about AutoCorrect options or if you want to change or modify an AutoCorrect setting, you can open the **AutoCorrect** dialog box. You also use this dialog box to add your own AutoCorrect entry.

Besides replacing misspellings and abbreviations, you can also find and replace other text. If you know that you want to substitute one word or phrase for another, you can use the **Find and Replace** dialog box to find each occurrence of the word that you want to change and replace it with another. On the **Replace** tab of the **Find and Replace** dialog box, use the **Find Next** button to locate the next occurrence of the text that you enter in the **Find what** box and then use the **Replace** button to replace the text that you found with the text in the **Replace with** box. You can use the **Replace** button to continue to replace each occurrence individually, the **Replace All** button to replace all of the occurrences, or the **Find Next** button to locate the next occurrence. If you want to only find text and not replace it, you can use the **Find** tab in the **Find and Replace** dialog box and use the **Find Next** button. You can access the **Find and Replace** commands on the **Edit** menu.

Replace Text

In this exercise, you change an AutoCorrect setting, add an AutoCorrect entry and change text as you type. You also find a phrase and replace it with another one throughout the entire document.

Open

1   On the Standard toolbar, click the **Open** button.

The **Open** dialog box appears.

2   Navigate to the **SBS** folder on your hard disk, double-click the **Word** folder, double- click the **CreatingDoc** folder and then double-click the **ReplaceText** file.

The ReplaceText document opens.

3   On the **Tools** menu, click **AutoCorrect Options**.

The **AutoCorrect** dialog box appears, displaying the **AutoCorrect** tab.

4   Clear the **Capitalize first letter of sentences** check box so that Word will not capitalize a letter or word that follows a period.

5   Click in the **Replace** box and then type **gc**.

6   Press the ⌈Tab⌋ key to move the insertion point in the **With** box.

7   Type **The Garden Company**.

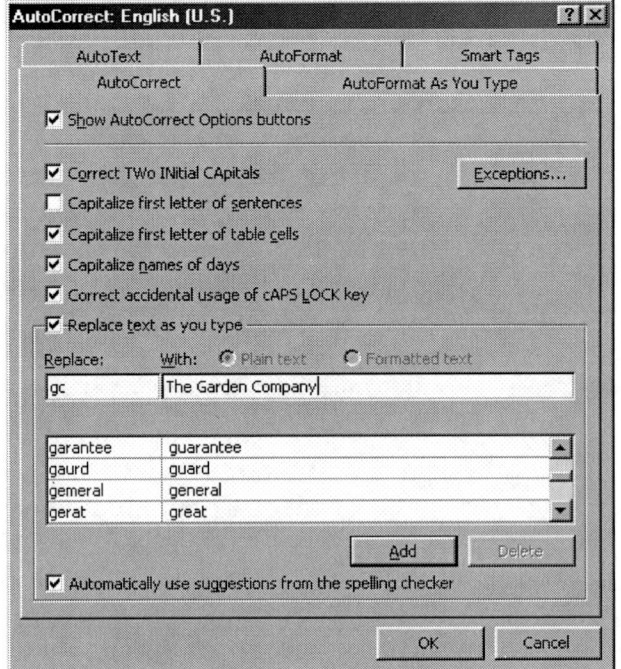

8   Click **Add** to add the entry to the correction list.

The text for the new AutoCorrect entry will be displayed each time you type its abbreviation and press [Space].

9   Click **OK** to close the **AutoCorrect** dialog box.

10   Press [Ctrl] **+** [End] to place the insertion point at the end of the document.

11   Type **gc** and then press [Space].

The text *gc* changes to *The Garden Company*.

12   Press [Ctrl] **+** [Home] to move the insertion point to the beginning of the document.

13   On the **Edit** menu, click **Replace**.

The **Find and Replace** dialog box appears.

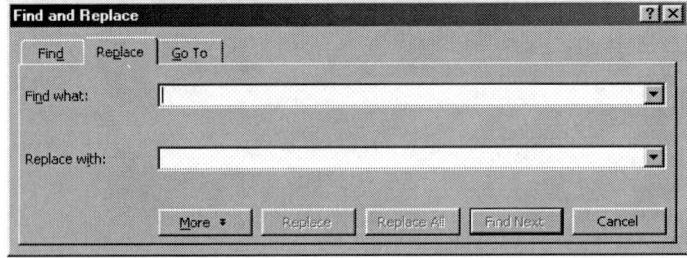

14   In the **Find what** box, type **Garden Map Kit** and then press [Tab] to move the insertion point in the **Replace with** box.

15   In the **Replace with** box, type **Interactive Garden** and then click **Find Next**.

Word finds and selects the first mention of *Garden Map Kit*.

16   Click **Replace**.

The selection is replaced with the text *Interactive Garden* and the next occurrence is selected.

17 Click **Replace All**.

The Word message box that appears indicates that nine replacements were made.

18 Click **OK** and then click **Close** to close the **Find and Replace** dialog box.

19 On the Standard toolbar, click the **Save** button to save the document.

Close

20 Click the **Close Window** button in the document window.

The ReplaceText document closes.

Lesson Wrap-Up

To finish this lesson:

Close

1 On the **File** menu, click **Exit**, or click the **Close** button in the Word window.

Word closes.

Quick Quizzes

● How do you start Word?

● How do you create a new document?

● How do you open an existing document?

● Which of these statements about "save" and "save as" are true?

  • "Save As" allows you to change the name or the location of an existing file.

  • There is no difference when you save the file for the first time:

  • "Save" is used to accept changes made to an existing file.

● What is the Office Assistant?

● What does the Undo button do?

● What do you use the Office Clipboard for?

● What do you use the Select Browse Object button for?

LESSON 2

Changing the Look of Text in a Document

You want your documents to look professional-well designed and polished. The appearance of your text should reflect the content of your message. The format of your paragraphs and pages influences the appeal of your documents and helps draw the reader's attention to important information. To enhance the appearance of your documents, you can format the text to make your words stand out and arrange paragraphs to make them easy to read.

In this lesson, you'll improve the appearance of the text in a document by changing text characteristics, or **attributes**. You can change the text by making it bold, italic, or coloured. You'll also change the appearance of the paragraphs in a document by indenting and changing the alignment and by setting tab stops for lines within paragraphs. Finally, you'll create and modify bulleted and numbered lists.

This lesson uses the practice files FormatText, FormatAuto, FormatPara and CreateList that you installed from this book's CD-ROM. For details about installing the practice files, see "Using the Book's CD-ROM" at the beginning of this book.

Changing the Appearance of Text

W2002-1-2
W2002-1-4

The text that you type in a document appears in a font typeface. A **font typeface**, or simply **font**, is a complete set of characters that uses the same design. Depending on your printer, the fonts available on your computer may vary. Some fonts, such as Times New Roman, Courier and Arial, are fairly common. In addition to the design, the size of each character is also part of the font. The **font size** of text is measured in **points**. A point is equal to about 1/72 of an inch.

It is possible to increase or decrease the font size by half-points by typing the font size directly in the **Font Size** box and pressing **Enter** (for example, you can enter a font size of 12.5).

You can emphasize text using special **font effects**, such as bold type, italics, all capital letters, or shadows. For example, to make a heading stand out, you could make it bold. To draw attention to a warning, you could make it italic. You can also add emphasis by changing the colour of the text in your document. For example, you could use white text on a black or grey background. If you plan to print your documents on a colour printer or send them electronically, you can apply other colours to the text and its background.

Reveal Formatting task pane new for **Office**XP

When you are formatting a document, you can open the **Reveal Formatting** task pane to display the formatting of selected text, such as its font and font effects. The **Reveal Formatting** task pane allows you to display, change, or clear the formatting for the selected text. You also can use the **Reveal Formatting** task pane to select text based on formatting so that you can compare the formatting used in the selected text with formatting used in other parts of the document.

The Garden Company catalogue will include an article on lilies in its upcoming spring catalogue. The text in the document will be formatted to visually communicate the beauty of this type of flower.

Format Text

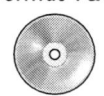

In this exercise, you change the font typeface, font size and font colour to format text in a document.

1 Start Word, if necessary.

Open

2 On the Standard toolbar, click the **Open** button.

The **Open** dialog box appears.

3 Navigate to the **SBS** folder on your hard disk, double-click the **Word** folder, double- click the **FormattingText** folder and then double-click the **FormatText** file.

The FormatText document opens.

4 Select the title *The Lovely Lily* at the top of the document.

5 On the Formatting toolbar, click the **Font** down arrow, scroll down in the list of available fonts and then click **Monotype Corsiva**.

troubleshooting

If Monotype Corsiva is not available, select a similar font, such as Brush Script MT.

The title at the top of the document now appears in a new font.

Font Size 12

6 On the Formatting toolbar, click the **Font Size** down arrow and then click **26** in the list.

The size of the title text is increased to 26 points.

7 On the **Format** menu, click **Reveal Formatting**.

The **Reveal Formatting** task pane appears, displaying the formatting of the selected text.

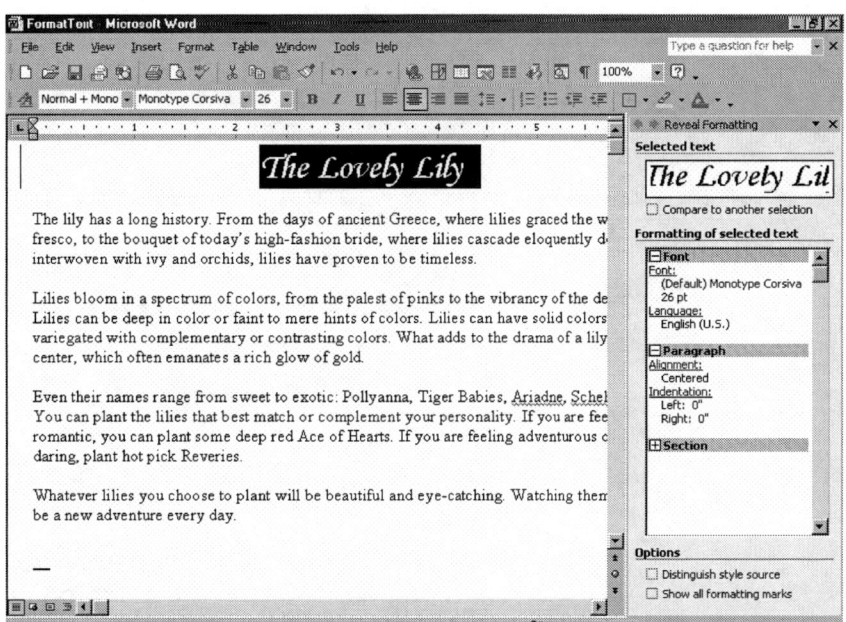

8   In the **Reveal Formatting** task pane, click the **Font** link in the **Font** section.

The **Font** dialog box appears.

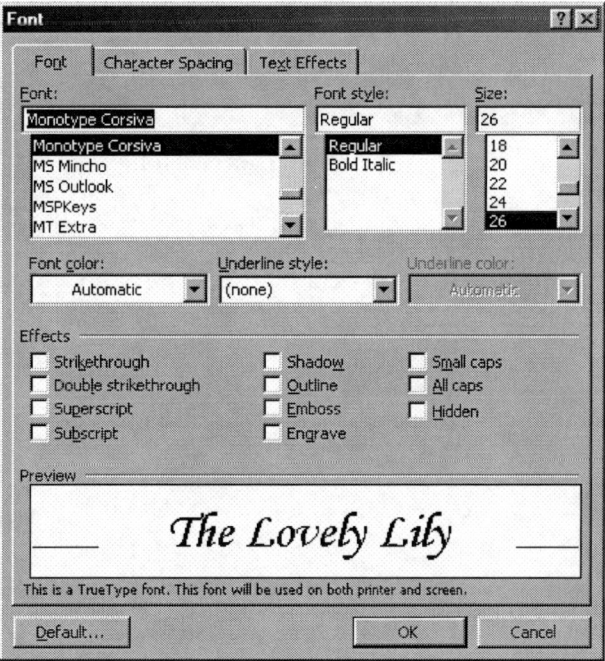

9   In the **Effects** area, select the **Outline** check box and then click **OK**.

The selected text appears with an outline effect and that effect is now listed in the **Reveal Formatting** task pane in the **Font** section.

10   In the **Reveal Formatting** task pane, point to the **Selected text** box at the top of the task pane.

A down arrow appears on the right side of the **Selected text** box.

11   In the **Selected text** box, click the down arrow and then click **Clear Formatting**.

The formatting for the selected text is removed.

Undo

12 On the Standard toolbar, click the **Undo** button.

The formatting for the selected text is restored.

13 Select the word *pinks* in the first sentence of the second paragraph.

Font Colour

14 On the Formatting toolbar, click the **Font Colour** down arrow and then click the **Pink** colour box (first column, fourth row) on the colour palette.

The colour of the selected word is now pink and the formatting is listed in the **Font** section of the **Reveal Formatting** task pane.

tip

To apply the most recently selected colour to other text, select the word or phrase and then click the **Font Colour** button (not the down arrow). The colour that appears on the **Font Colour** button is applied to the selected text.

Highlight

15 Select the phrase *rich glow of gold* at the end of the second paragraph, click the **Highlight** down arrow on the Formatting toolbar and then click the **Yellow** colour box (first column, first row).

The highlighted phrase now stands out from the rest of the text.

Highlighting pointer

tip

You do not have to select the text first before choosing a highlighting colour. You can select a highlighting colour from the colour palette and then use the highlighting pointer to highlight the text.

16 Scroll to the right and then select the text *Pollyanna, Tiger Babies, Ariadne, Scheharazade* in the third paragraph.

troubleshooting

If the **Reveal Formatting** task pane overlays some of the text in the document, you can resize the task pane. Position the pointer over the left edge of the task pane and when the pointer changes to the double arrow pointer, drag the edge to the right so that the text of the document is visible.

17 On the **Format** menu, click **Font** to open the **Font** dialog box, select the **Small caps** check box and then click **OK**.

The lowercase letters in the names of the lilies now appear in small caps, making those names easier to find in the text.

18 In the same paragraph, select the text *Ace of Hearts* and then hold down the `Ctrl` key and double-click the text *Reveries* in the last line of the paragraph to select the nonadjacent text.

19 Press the `F4` key.

The other lily names appear in small caps. When you press `F4`, the change that you just made is applied to the selected text.

20 In the **Reveal Formatting** task pane, point to the **Selected text** box, click the down arrow and then click **Select All Text With Similar Formatting**.

All the flower names that have been formatted in small caps are selected.

Bold

B

21 On the Formatting toolbar, click the **Bold** button.

The flower names are now bold.

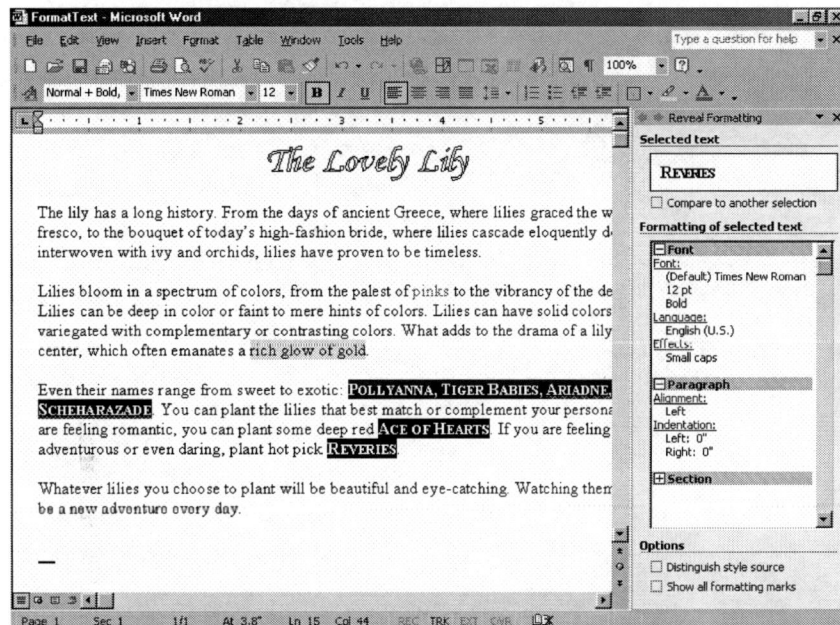

Close

✕

22 In the **Reveal Formatting** task pane, click the **Close** button.

The **Reveal Formatting** task pane closes.

23 On the Standard toolbar, click the **Save** button to save the document.

Close

✕

24 Click the **Close Window** button in the document window.

The FormatText document closes.

Adding Animation to Text

If someone using a computer will be reading your document, you can add effects that will make the text in your document vibrant and visually alive. You can apply sparkling and flashing lights or a marquee that will draw your reader's attention to specific words and phrases in the document. To add these special effects, you can apply an animation to selected text in your document.

To add animation to selected text:

1 Select the text that you want to animate.

2 On the **Format** menu, click **Font**.

The **Font** dialog box appears.

3 Click the **Text Effects** tab.

4 In the **Animations** box, select the animation effect that you want to add to the selected text.

5 Click **OK**.

Formatting Text as You Type

W2002-1-2
W2002-1-5
W2002-1-1

To get a list of AutoText entries, you can print them by clicking **AutoText entries** on the **Print what** drop-down list in the **Print** dialog box.

Word provides automated formatting tools that let you enter and format text as you type. Word's **AutoText** feature can save you time and create consistency in your documents by providing standardized text for commonly used items, such as attention line entries, closings and mailing instructions, that you want to insert in your document and by allowing you to create AutoText entries for words and phrases that you use repeatedly, such as your name, address, company and job title. To insert one of the built-in AutoText entries, such as the closing of a letter, you click the **Insert** menu, point to **AutoText**, point to a category, such as **Closing** and then select the closing (for example, *Respectfully yours,*) that you want to insert in your document. You can also create your own AutoText entries using the **AutoText** tab in the **AutoCorrect** dialog box. For example, you can create an AutoText entry for *Catherine Turner*, the owner of The Garden Company. Once the AutoText entry is stored, you can type the first four letters of the name *Catherine* and a ScreenTip will display *Catherine Turner (Press ENTER to Insert)*. Then to insert the AutoText entry in the document, you press ⌷ Enter ⌷ and continue typing. If you don't want to insert the AutoText entry (that is, if you are inserting someone else's name), you just press ⌷ Space ⌷ and continue typing.

In addition to automating text entry, Word can also automate formatting as you type with a tool called **AutoFormat**. For example, instead of manually creating a line by typing underscores (_) across the length of a page, you can type just a few equal signs (=) or dashes (-). When you type three consecutive equal signs and press ⌷ Enter ⌷, Word creates a double-line border; when you type three consecutive dashes and press ⌷ Enter ⌷, Word creates a single-line border.

Besides commonly used words and phrases, you can also insert symbols, special characters and the date and the time. Certain kinds of documents require special characters or symbols, such as a degree symbol (°) or a copyright symbol (©). If the documents that you create are time-sensitive, you can insert the current date and time. You can even choose to have Word update the date and time when you open the document. Word uses your computer's internal calendar and clock as its source.

Smart Tags
new for
OfficeXP

When you type certain information, such as the date and time, personal names, places, telephone numbers, or recent Microsoft Outlook e-mail recipients, Word recognizes the information and displays a **Smart Tag**, a dotted line under the text. A Smart Tag provides options for commonly performed tasks associated with the information. For example, you can add a name and address that you just typed in a Word document to your Contacts list in Microsoft Outlook. To do this, you point to the name in the document, click the **Smart Tag Actions** button and then click **Add to Contacts** from the list of available Smart Tag options.

FormatAuto

In this exercise, you insert decorative design symbols in a document, insert one of the standard closings provided by Word, create an AutoText entry and insert it in the document and add a double border using an AutoFormat shortcut. You also insert the date and examine actions that you can take using Smart Tags.

Open

1   On the Standard toolbar, click the **Open** button.

The **Open** dialog box appears.

2   Navigate to the SBS folder on your hard disk, double-click the **Word** folder, double- click the **FormattingText** folder and then double-click **FormatAuto**.

The FormatAuto document opens.

3   Press the End key to place the insertion point at the end of the first line of text and then press Enter to insert a blank new line.

4   On the **Insert** menu, click **Symbol**.

The **Symbol** dialog box appears.

5   Click the **Font** down arrow, scroll to the bottom of the list and then click **Wingdings2**.

tip

The Wingdings fonts are sets of specials characters, shapes, symbols and thumbprint-sized pictures that you can insert in the text of your documents to draw attention to the message that you are trying to convey. The following are examples of the Wingdings character set: ▣ ♉ ◔ ☺.

6   Scroll to the fifth row and then click the decorative design symbol located in the sixth column and in the fifth row with a character code of *101*, as shown in the following illustration.

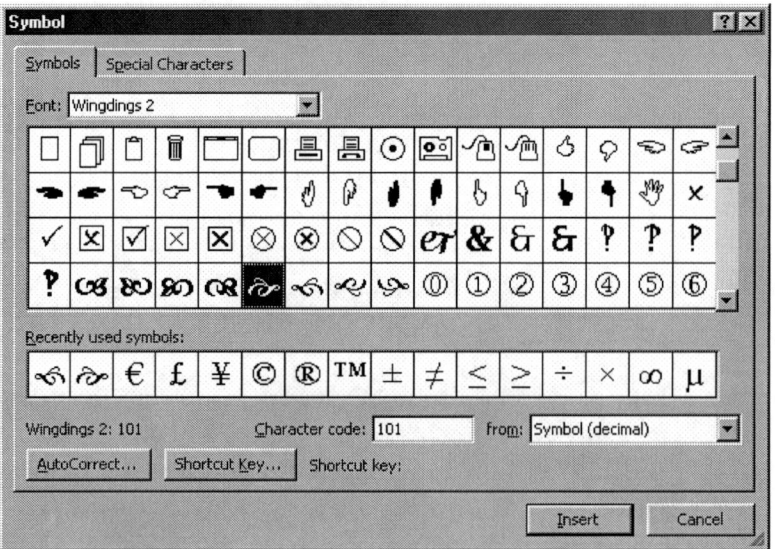

7 Click **Insert**.

The decorative design symbol is inserted below the title of the document.

8 Click the decorative design symbol located in the seventh column in the fifth row with a character code of *102*, click **Insert** and then click **Close**.

The second decorative symbol appears in the document.

tip

You can automatically format a document as you type using the options in the **AutoFormat As You Type** tab in the **AutoCorrect** dialog box or you can format a document after you type using the **AutoFormat** command on the **Format** menu. In the **AutoFormat** dialog box, click the **AutoFormat now** option or the **AutoFormat and review each change** option and then click **OK**.

9 Press ⌈Ctrl⌋ ✛ ⌈End⌋ to move the insertion point to the end of the document.

10 On the **Insert** menu, point to **AutoText**, point to **Closing** and then click **Respectfully,** to insert this standard closing text at the location of the insertion point.

11 Press ⌈Enter⌋ four times to leave space for a signature.

12 On the **Insert** menu, point to **AutoText** and then click **AutoText**.

The **AutoCorrect** dialog box appears.

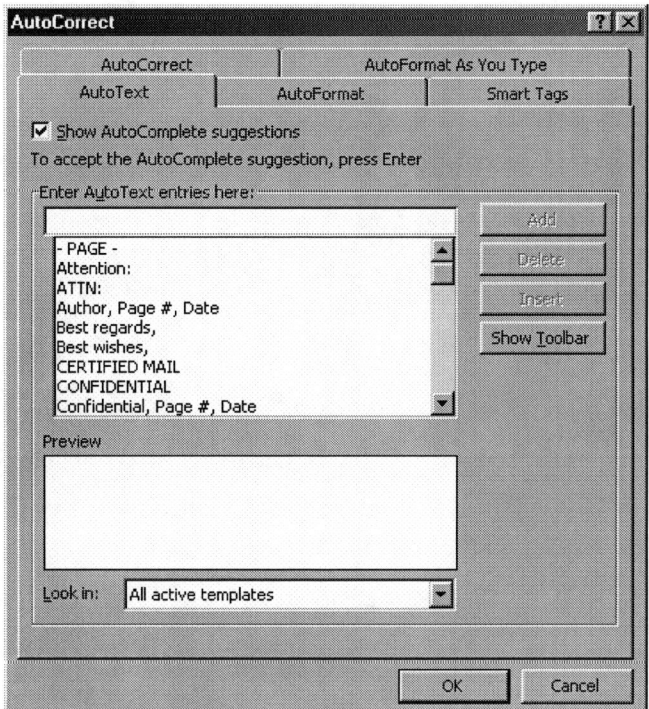

13 In the **Enter AutoText entries here** box, type **Catherine Turner**, click **Add** and then click **OK**.

The **AutoCorrect** dialog box closes and the AutoText entry is stored.

14 Type **Cath**.

The ScreenTip displays *Catherine Turner (Press ENTER to Insert)*.

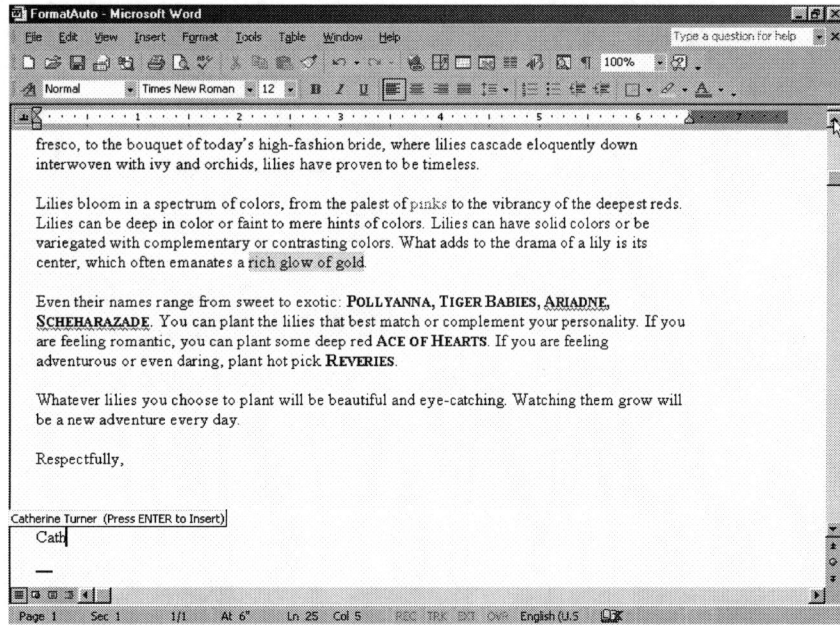

15 Press Enter to insert the full name and then press Enter twice to insert two blank lines.

16 Press [+=] three times and then press Enter .

A double border appears. The **AutoCorrect Options** button appears just above the double border. No modifications are needed.

tip

The **AutoCorrect Options** button provides options related to the AutoCorrect border that you have just inserted. You can choose to remove the border, disable (or turn off) the AutoCorrect border lines options, or open the **AutoCorrect** dialog box, in which you can make further modifications to this feature.

17   On the **Insert** menu, click **Date and Time**.

The **Date and Time** dialog box appears.

18   Click today's date with the **dd month yyyy** format, such as 15 March 2003.

19   Click **OK** to enter the current date in the document and then press ⌈ Enter ⌋ to insert a blank line.

Smart Tag Actions   **20**   Point to the date to display the **Smart Tag Actions** button and then click the **Smart Tag Actions** button.

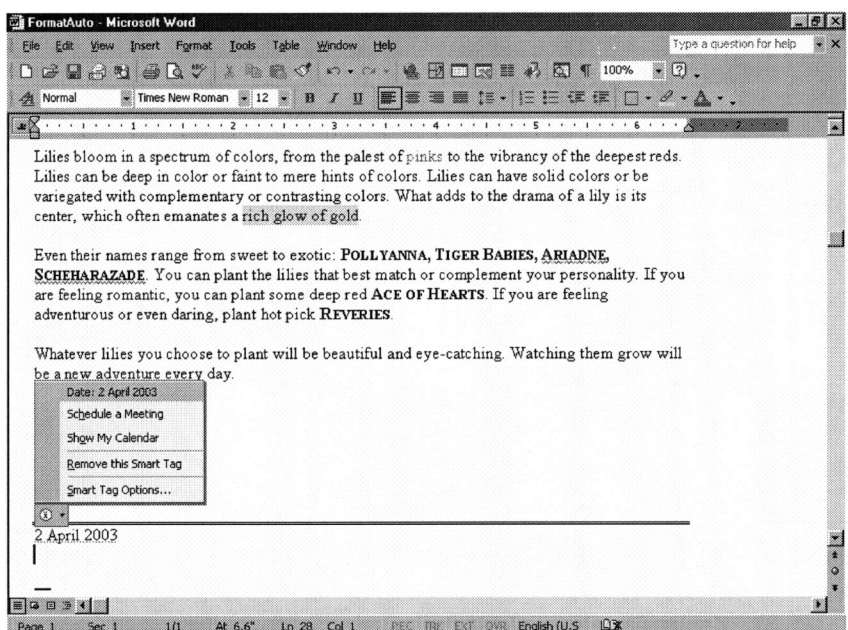

21   On the menu, click **Smart Tag Options**.

The **AutoCorrect** dialog box appears, displaying the **Smart Tags** tab.

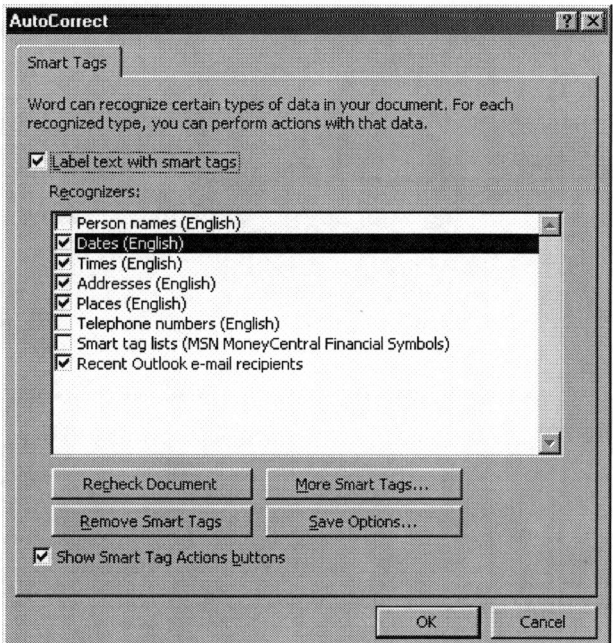

You can use this dialog box to turn on and off the Smart Tags feature. Do not turn off the feature at this time.

22 Click **OK** to close the **AutoCorrect** dialog box.

23 On the Standard toolbar, click the **Save** button to save the document.

24 Click the **Close Window** button in the document window.

The FormatAuto document closes.

Close

Changing the Appearance of a Paragraph

W2002-2-1
W2002-2-2

You can enhance the appearance of a paragraph by changing the way text is aligned, modifying the spacing between paragraphs and adding borders and shading around text. In Word, a **paragraph** is any amount of text that ends when you press the [Enter] key. A paragraph can include several sentences or a single line of text consisting of one or more words.

You control the length of a line by setting the left and right margins and the length of a page by setting the top and bottom margins. The width of a margin controls the amount of white space that surrounds your text. You can use the options in the **Page Setup** dialog box to control the margins in the document.

To have a more professional-looking document, you can select the **Mirror margins** option on the **Page Setup** dialog box.

After you've set up a document's margins, you can control the positioning of the text within the margins. In Word, you can align lines of text in different locations along the horizontal ruler using tab stops. You can also indent paragraphs. When you indent a paragraph, you control where the first line of text begins, where the second and subsequent lines begin and where paragraph text wraps at the right margin.

You use the horizontal ruler, which you can display at the top of the Word document window, to set **tab stops**. Tab stops are locations along the ruler that you use to align text. By default, the tab stops in Word are set at every half-inch mark on the ruler. To set a tab using the ruler, you click the tab indicator, which is a button with a symbol on it, located at the left end of the ruler. Each time you click the tab indicator, a different type of tab stop indicator appears. When the type of tab stop that you want to set appears, you click the ruler where you want to set the tab. To remove a tab stop, you drag it down and away from the ruler.

After you set a tab stop, you position the insertion point to the left of the text you want to align and then press the [Tab] key. The text is aligned along the next tab stop. For example, if you set a center tab, when you press [Tab], the text moves to the right and aligns itself using the center tab stop as the middle point. A decimal tab aligns numbers on their decimal points.

tip

In Word, you can display formatting marks to help you align and space the text in a document correctly. Formatting marks do not print with your document. They are displayed in your document just as an aid. To turn on formatting marks, click the **Show/Hide ¶** button on the Standard toolbar. Examples of formatting marks include the paragraph mark ¶, which marks the end of a paragraph and the tab stop (→), which marks the location of a tab stop. To turn off the display of formatting marks, click the **Show/Hide ¶** button again.

In addition to tab stops, the horizontal ruler also includes special markers that you can use to control how text wraps on the left or right side of a document. You use these markers if you want to **indent** the text toward the right or left. To indent text, you can use one of the indent markers located on the horizontal ruler. The following table describes each indent marker:

Marker on Ruler	Icon	Description
First Line Indent	▽	Sets where the first line of text in a paragraph begins.
Hanging Indent	△	Sets where the second and all subsequent lines of text wrap after reaching the right margin.
Left Indent	▭	Sets where the text indents when you press [Tab].
Right Indent	△	Sets where the text wraps as it reaches the right margin. By default, the right indent marker is set at the right margin, but you can change that setting.

When you use the ruler to format paragraphs, you can use Print Layout view to see how far your page margins are from the borders of the page. Print Layout view also shows two rulers: the horizontal ruler at the top and the vertical ruler along the left side of the document window. The vertical ruler helps you adjust the top and bottom margins in the document.

You can also position text within the document's margin using the alignment buttons on the Formatting toolbar. Click the **Align Left** button to align text along the left margin, click the **Align Right** button to align the text along the right margin, click the **Center** button to align a paragraph between the left and right margins and click the **Justify** button to align between the margins, creating a flush-right edge for the text.

To add space between paragraphs, you can press ⎡ Enter ⎤ to insert a blank line. For more precise control, you can adjust the spacing before and after paragraphs. For example, instcad of indicating a new paragraph by indenting the first line, you could create a more professional appearance by adding twelve points of blank space before a new paragraph. You use the **Paragraph** dialog box to adjust the paragraph spacing.

To set off a paragraph from the rest of the document, you can add borders and shading. For example, if you are sending a long letter to a client, you can place a border around the paragraph that you want the client to pay the most attention to. You can also shade the background of a paragraph to create a subtler effect.

After you indent, align, space, border, or shade one paragraph, you can press ⎡ Enter ⎤ to apply these same effects to the next paragraph that you type. To apply the effects to an existing paragraph, you can use the Format Painter to quickly copy the format of one paragraph to another.

The Garden Company catalogue includes an announcement, which needs to be formatted to fit the layout of the catalogue and match its new colour design.

In this exercise, you modify text alignment, insert and modify tab stops, modify line spacing and add borders and shading around text to change the appearance of the paragraphs in the document.

1   On the Standard toolbar, click the **Open** button.

     The **Open** dialog box appears.

2   Navigate to the **SBS** folder on your hard disk, double-click the **Word** folder, double- click the **FormattingText** folder and then double-click the **FormatPara** file.

     The FormatPara document opens.

To change the margins of a document, display the **Page Setup** dialog box by holding down the **Alt** key and double-clicking the *Ruler*

To copy a format more than once, double-click the **Format Painter** button on the **Standard Toolbar** and then click on each paragraph you want to apply the format to. To deactivate the option, click the **Format Painter** button again or press **Esc**

FormatPara

Open

Print Layout View

3   Click the **Print Layout View** button.

The document view changes. You can see how the work area is aligned between the left and right margins. In addition to the horizontal ruler at the top of the document window, a vertical ruler also appears on the left side of the document window.

White space between pages
new for

tip

In Print Layout view, you can show or hide the white space between the pages. Position the pointer between the pages until the Show White Space pointer or Hide White Space pointer appears and then click the page.

Show/Hide
¶

4   On the Standard toolbar, click the **Show/Hide ¶** button to display the formatting marks.

5   Click immediately to the left of the word *for* in the title, hold down the [Shift] key and then press [Enter].

Part of the title wraps to the second line of text.

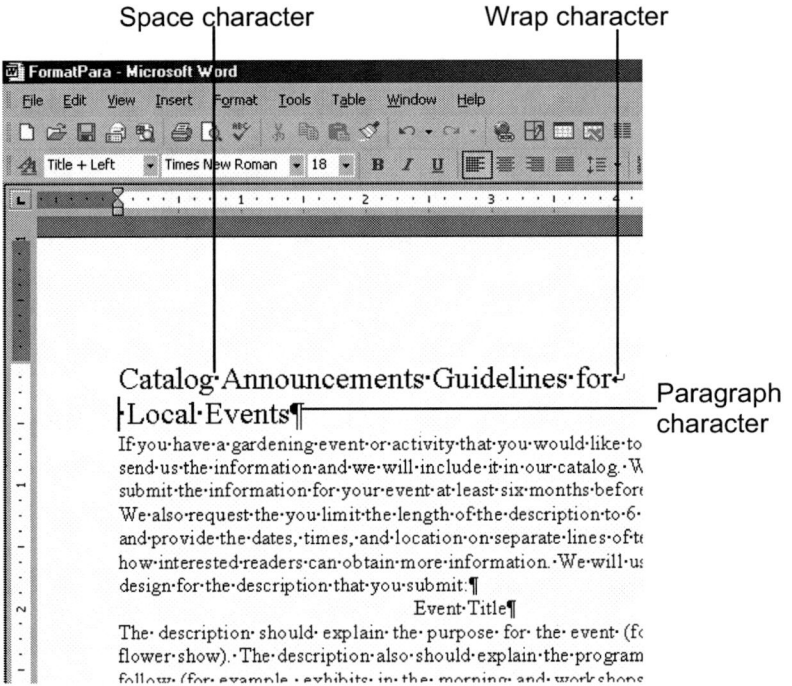

Center
≣

6   On the Formatting toolbar, click the **Center** button to center the title to make it appear more balanced.

Justify
≣

7   Click anywhere in the first paragraph and then click the **Justify** button on the Formatting toolbar.

The paragraph is now formatted with the text flush against both left and right margins.

First Line Indent
▽

8   Drag the **First Line Indent** marker to the 0.5-inch mark on the horizontal ruler.

The first line of text in the paragraph is indented a half inch from the left margin.

Left Indent

9   Click anywhere in the paragraph that starts with the text *The description should explain* and then drag the **Left Indent** marker to the 0.5-inch mark on the horizontal ruler.

The paragraph is indented on the left side.

Right Indent
⌂

10 Drag the **Right Indent** marker to the 5-inch mark on the ruler.

The paragraph now appears indented on the right side as well.

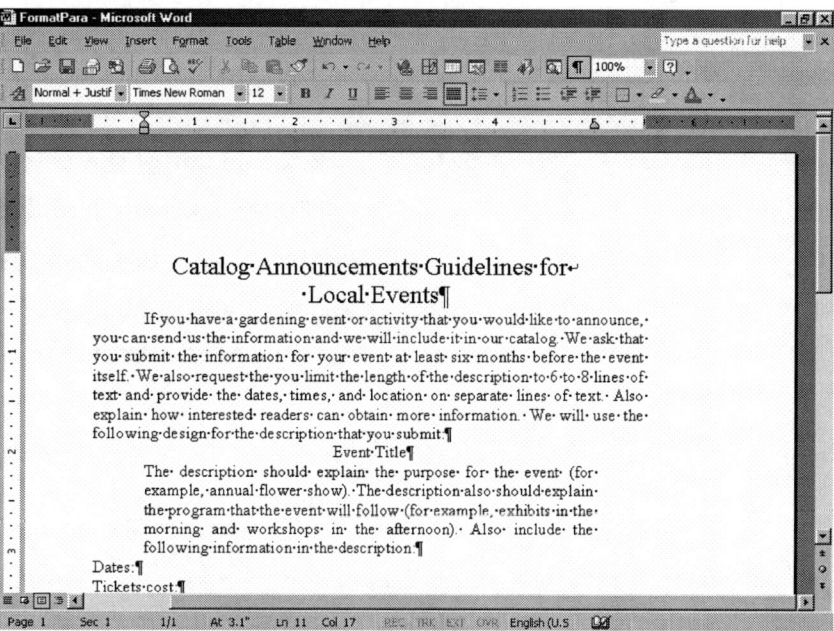

Left Tab icon
L

11 Scroll down the page, select the two lines that include the text *Dates:* and *Tickets cost:*, make sure that the **Tab Indicator** button shows the **Left Tab** icon and then click the ruler at the 1-inch mark to set a left tab.

12 Click to the left of the word *Dates* to deselect all the text and then press Tab to align the text at the new tab stop.

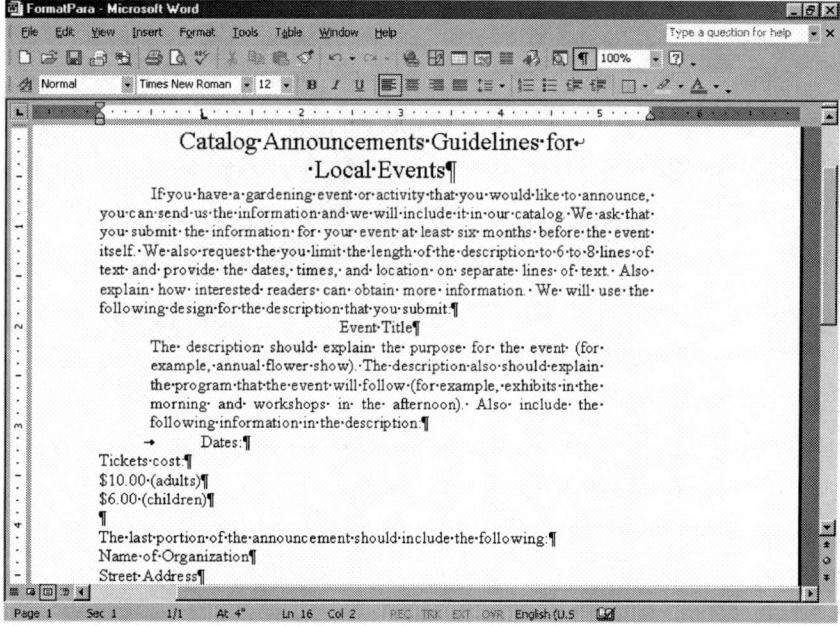

13 Press End to move the insertion point to the end of the line and then press Enter to create a new line. Press Tab and then type Times:.

14   Press ⎡Enter⎤ to create a new line, press ⎡Tab⎤, type Location:, press the ⎡→⎤ key to move the insertion point to the beginning of the next line and then press ⎡Tab⎤.

Decimal Tab icon
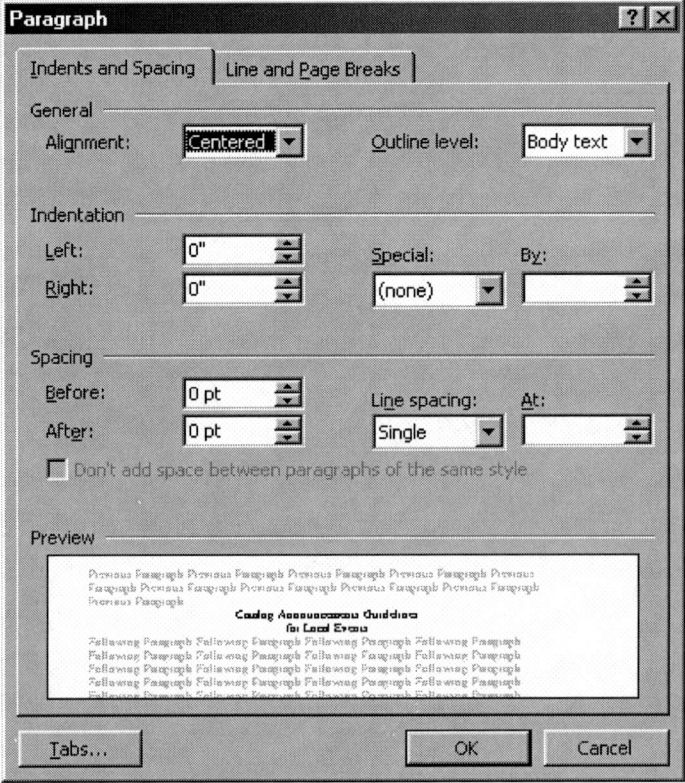

15   Select the two lines that start with text *$10.00* and *$6.00*, click the **Tab Indicator** three times to see a **Decimal Tab** icon and then click the ruler at the 2.5-inch mark to set a decimal tab.

16   Click to the left of the text *$10.00 to deselect the text*, press ⎡Tab⎤, click to the left of the text *$6.00* and then press ⎡Tab⎤.

The dollar amounts are aligned along their decimal points.

17   Select the two lines of text with the dollar amounts again and drag the decimal tab from the 2.5-inch mark to the 2.0-inch mark to adjust the tab stop.

18   Press ⎡Ctrl⎤ **+** ⎡Home⎤ to move the insertion point to the top of the document and then on the **Format** menu, click **Paragraph**.

The **Paragraph** dialog box appears.

tip

You can also use the **Paragraph** dialog box to control the left and right indentation instead of using the ruler.

19   In the **Spacing** area, click the **After** up arrow two times to display *12 pt* and then click **OK**.

The paragraphs below the title move down. The added space helps to set the title off from the rest of the document.

Format Painter

20   On the Standard toolbar, click the **Format Painter** button, move the mouse pointer to the paragraph that begins *Event Title* and then click the text to copy the formatting from the title paragraph.

Additional spacing appears between the first paragraph and the *Event Title* text and the font size changes to 18 points.

21   On the **Format** menu, click **Paragraph** to open the **Paragraph** dialog box. In the **Spacing** area, click the **Before** up arrow twice to display *12 pt* and then click **OK**.

There is more spacing between the *Event Title* text and the paragraph before it.

Center

22   Scroll down the page, select the last four lines of text in the document, which start with the line *The last portion of* and then on the Formatting toolbar, click the **Center** button to center these lines of text.

23   On the **Format** menu, click **Borders and Shading**.

The **Borders and Shading** dialog box appears, displaying the **Borders** tab.

24   In the **Setting** area, click the **Shadow** icon to select that border style.

25   Click the **Shading** tab, click the **Light Yellow** colour box on the colour palette (third column, last row) and then click **OK**.

A border with a shadow surrounds the text and the background colour is light yellow.

26   Click a blank area two lines below the yellow shaded box and then move the pointer to the center of the line until it changes shape.

Align center pointer

The pointer shape changes to the Click and Type's Align center pointer to indicate that when you click and type, the text will be centred.

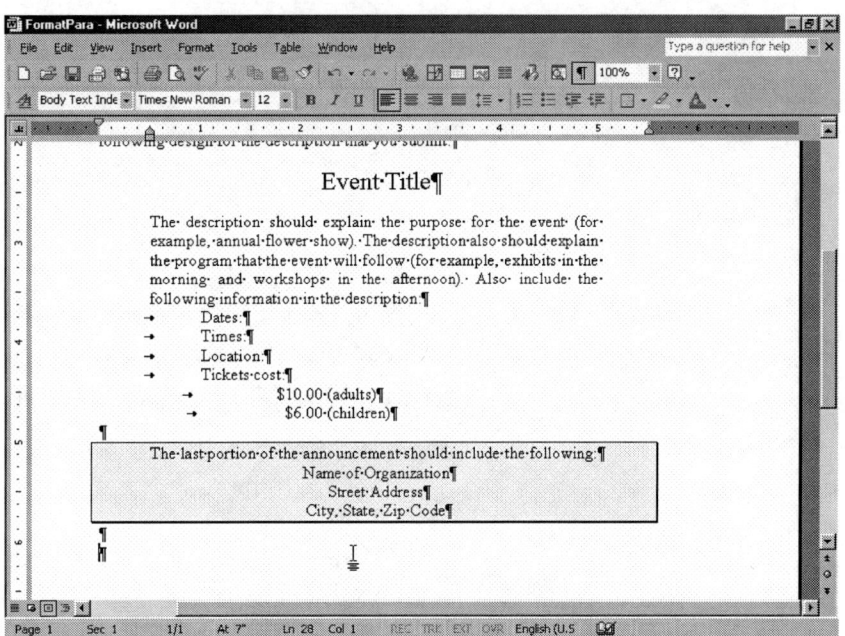

Show/Hide

¶

27 When the pointer changes shape, double-click to position the insertion point and then type **All announcements must be submitted 6 months in advance.**

The newly inserted text appears centred in the document.

28 On the Formatting toolbar, click the **Show/Hide ¶** button to hide the formatting marks.

29 On the Standard toolbar, click the **Save** button to save the document.

Close

☒

30 Click the **Close Window** button in the document window.

The FormatPara document closes.

W2002-2-3
W2002e-1-2

Creating and Modifying a List

To organize lists in your document, such as lists of events, names, numbers, or procedures, you can format the information in a bulleted or numbered list. A **bullet** is a small graphic, such as a large dot, that sets off an item in a list. Use numbers instead of bullets when you want to emphasize sequence, as in a series of steps. If you move, insert, or delete items in a numbered list, Word renumbers the list for you. If the items in a list are out of order, alphabetically or numerically, you can sort the items in ascending or descending order using the **Sort** command on the **Table** menu.

> You can change the colour of the numbers or bullets in a list by clicking **Customize** on the **Bullets and Numbering** dialog box.

For emphasis, you can change any bullet or number style to one of Word's predefined formats. For example, you can switch round bullets to check boxes, or Roman numerals to lowercase letters. You can also customise the list style or insert a picture as a bullet. Use the **Bullets and Numbering** dialog box to modify, format and customise your list.

> When you select a list, the numbers or bullets are not highlighted.

Word makes it easy to start a bulleted or numbered list. For a bulleted list, you simply click at the beginning of a line, type * (an asterisk) and then press [Space] or [Tab]; for a numbered list, you type **1.**, press [Space] or [Tab], type the first item in the list and then press [Enter]. The next bullet or number in the list appears and Word changes the formatting to a list. You can type the next item in the list or press [Enter] or [Backspace] to end the list.

You can change a bulleted or numbered list into an outline or create one of your own. Outlines are useful for organizing information, such as topics in an essay. An outline typically consists of main headings and subheadings. To start an outline, you click at the beginning of a line, type **I.**, press [Tab], type a main heading and then press [Enter]. You can type another main heading or press [Tab] to add a subheading under the main heading.

The Garden Company needs to complete the announcement that will be used on the back pages of the catalogue.

CreateList

Open

In this exercise, you create a bulleted and numbered list, modify it by adjusting its indents and then apply outline numbering.

1   On the Standard toolbar, click the **Open** button.

The **Open** dialog box appears.

2   Navigate to the **SBS** folder on your hard disk, double-click the **Word** folder, double- click the **FormattingText** folder and then double-click the **CreateList** file.

The CreateList document opens.

3   Select the four lines that start with the word *Dates*.

Numbering

4   On the Formatting toolbar, click the **Numbering** button.

The selected text appears as a numbered list.

5   On the **Format** menu, click **Bullets and Numbering**.

The **Bullets and Numbering** dialog box appears, displaying the **Numbered** tab.

You can select different symbols for a list's bullets by clicking **Customize** on the **Bullets and Numbering** dialog box.

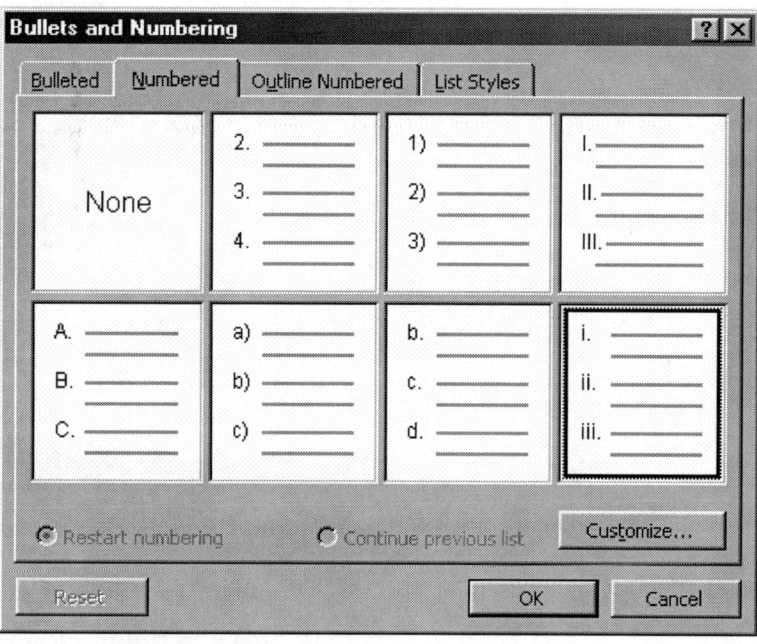

6   Click the A, B, C box (first column, second row) and then click **OK**.

The numbered list changes from numbers to letters.

7   Select the two lines that start with the text *$10.00* and *$6.00*.

Bullets

8   On the Formatting toolbar, click the **Bullets** button.

The selected text appears as a bulleted list.

Decrease Indent

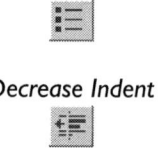

9   On the Formatting toolbar, click the **Decrease Indent** button.

The bulleted list is indented to the left and becomes part of the list.

List Styles
new for
OfficeXP

tip

You can define a style for a bulleted or numbered list to make one list look like another. On the **Format** menu, click **Bullets and Numbering**, click the **Styles** tab, click **New**, define the style and then click **OK**.

Increase Indent

10   On the Formatting toolbar, click the **Increase Indent** button.

The bulleted list is indented to the right and becomes a bulleted list again under the text *Tickets cost*.

11   On the **Format** menu, click **Bullets and Numbering**.

The **Bullets and Numbering** dialog box appears.

12   Click the **Bulleted** tab if necessary, click the colour bullet box (first column, second row) and then click **OK**.

The bullet character changes from circles to colours.

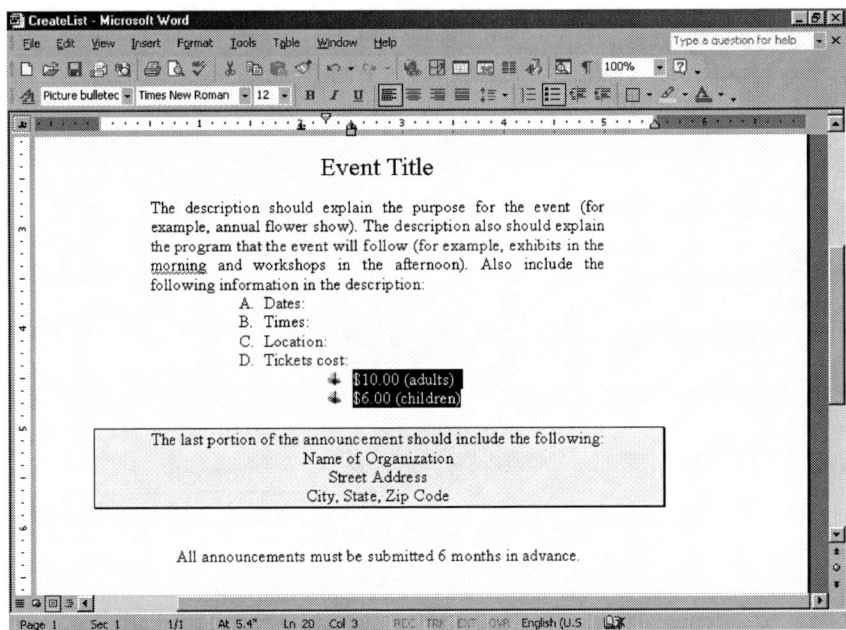

13   Select the six lines that start with the word *Dates*.

14   On the **Format** menu, click **Bullets and Numbering**.

The **Bullets and Numbering** dialog box appears.

15   Click the **Outline Numbered** tab if necessary, click the A Heading box (third column, second row) and then click **OK**.

The lettered list changes from letters to numbers and the bulleted list changes to letters.

16   On the Standard toolbar, click the **Save** button to save the document.

17   Click the **Close Window** button in the document window.

Close

The CreateList document closes.

Lesson Wrap-Up

To finish this lesson:

Close

1   On the **File** menu, click **Exit**, or click the **Close** button in the Word window.

Word closes.

Quick Quizzes

- What does formatting a document mean?

- How do you create an Autotext entry?

- What are tabs?

- How do you indent the first line of a paragraph?

- How do you change the line spacing in a paragraph?

- How do you set a document's margins?

- What do you use the Format Painter command for?

- How do you create a bulleted list?

- How do you create a document using a template?

LESSON 3 — Changing the Look of a Document

After completing this lesson, you will be able to:

✓ *Change the way each page appears in a document.*

✓ *Change the look of a document with styles.*

✓ *Change the look of a document with a theme.*

To draw a reader's attention to important information in a document, you can format the text so that it is visually appealing. The way that paragraphs in your document look can help to convey its message.

Word comes with formatting tools, such as templates, styles and themes, that you can use to enhance the appearance of your documents. You can change the characteristics, or attributes, of the text by applying bold formatting or italics to words and phrases or by changing the colour of the text that you type. You can also apply these visually enhancing attributes to paragraphs. To ensure a consistent and polished look for your document, you can apply those same attributes throughout your document.

In this lesson, you'll create a new template by modifying one of Word's templates. Then you will use the new template to create a fax cover page. You will also insert page and section breaks in a multiple-page document and make sure that the page breaks do not leave single words or phrases at the top or bottom of a page. You will change the way that the text is laid out on a page and you will add text that will appear at the top and bottom of every page in the document. Finally, you'll apply, modify and delete a formatting style using the **Styles and Formatting** task pane and then apply a theme to an existing document.

This lesson uses the practice files FormatPage and FormatStyle that you installed from this book's CD-ROM. For details about installing the practice files, see "Using the Book's CD-ROM" at the beginning of this book.

Changing the Design of a Document with Templates

W2002-4-2

The accuracy of the information in a document and the appearance of a document are both essential for effective communication. To help you create visually appealing documents, you can use one of Word's professionally designed templates.

A **template** is a special document that stores text, styles, formatting, macros and page information for use in other documents. You can start with a predefined Word template or use one that you create. Word comes with templates for all types of documents, including publications, reports, letters, faxes, memos and Web pages.

To create a document using one of Word's available templates, you click **New** on the **File** menu to display the **New Document** task pane. In the **New from template** section, click on **General Templates** to open the Templates dialog box, which contains several tabs that provide a wide range of templates from which to choose. When you create a document using a template, the document that appears on the screen displays placeholders that you use to enter your own text, or if you do not need the placeholders, you can delete them. A placeholder is surrounded by brackets. For example, *[click here and type name]* is one of the placeholders that appear in the document when you choose the Contemporary Fax template. To modify a placeholder, you click the placeholder text to select it and then enter your own text. Once you have entered the text that you need for the document, you can save the document. The template is not changed in any way. It is available to you to use for other documents.

You can also modify the templates to address professional and personal needs. In other words, you can create a document based on a template and then after entering your own text, such as your name and address, you can then save the modified document as another template. You can then use the template that you created instead of the ones provided by Word.

You can quickly try a new look by attaching a different template to your current document. The attached template's styles replace the styles in your document. To attach a template to an existing document, you click **Templates and Add-Ins** on the **Tools** menu, click **Attach** and then navigate to and open the template.

The Garden Company needs to send a fax to a supplier for review and confirmation of delivery of an order. Each fax that the company sends includes a fax cover page. The Garden Company uses one of Word's built-in templates but would rather have a template that already contains the company- specific information in place.

In this exercise, you create a new template based on an existing Word template. Then you create a fax cover page document using the new template.

1 Start Word, if necessary.

2 On the **View** menu, click **Task Pane**, if necessary, to display the **New Document** task pane.

3 In the **New Document** task pane, click **General Templates** in the **New from template** section to open the **Templates** dialog box.

4 Click the **Letters & Faxes** tab

5 Click the **Contemporary Fax** icon.

The template appears in the preview window.

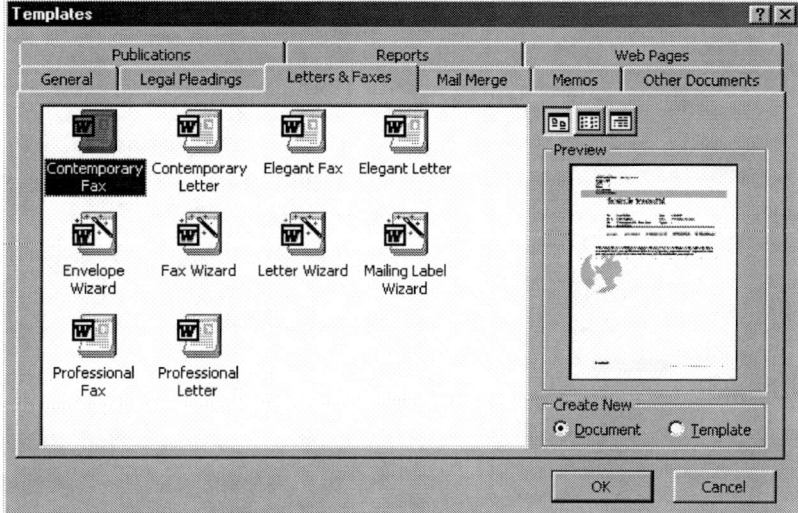

6 Click **OK**.

A new document with the template placeholders appears.

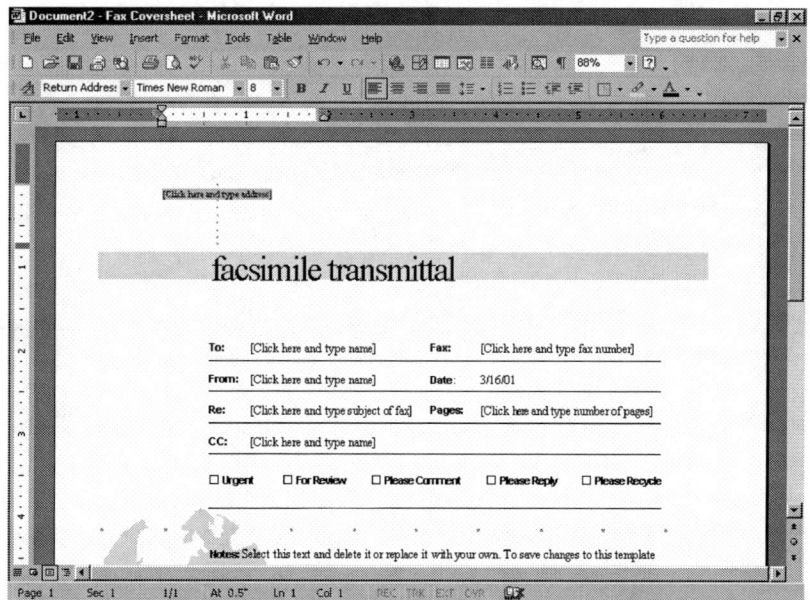

7 Click the placeholder *[Click here and type address]*, type **The Garden Company** and then press the ⎡ Enter ⎤ key.

8 Type **1234 Oak Street**, press ⎡ Enter ⎤ and then type **Seattle, WA 10101** to enter text in the placeholder.

9 Click the *From* placeholder *[Click here and type name]* and then type **The Garden Company** to replace the placeholder text with your own.

10 On the **File** menu, click **Save As**.

The **Save As** dialog box appears.

11 In the **File name** box, type **FaxTemplate**.

12 Click the **Save as type** down arrow and then click **Document Template**.

13 Navigate to the **Windows** folder on your hard disk, double- click the **Application Data** folder, double-click the **Microsoft** folder and then double-click the **Templates** folder.

14 Click **Save**.

Word saves the template; it will appear as an icon on the **General** tab in the **Templates** dialog box along with the other Word templates.

Close

15 Click the **Close Window** button in the document window.

The FaxTemplate closes.

16 On the **File** menu, click **New**.

The **New Document** task pane appears.

17 In the **New Document** task pane, click **General Templates** in the **New from template** section.

The **Templates** dialog box appears.

18 Click the **General** tab, click the **FaxTemplate** icon and then click **OK**.

The company-specific template appears in the document window.

19 Click the *To* placeholder *[Click here and type name]* and then type **Flower Supplier**.

20 Click the *Fax* placeholder *[Click here and type fax number]* and then type **1-800-555-0190**.

21 Click the *Re* placeholder *[Click here and type subject of fax]* and then type **Order Confirmation**.

22 Click the *Pages* placeholder *[Click here and type number of pages]* and then type **2**.

23 Click the *CC* placeholder *[Click here and type name]* and then press the ⃞Del⃞ key.

24 Select the paragraph that starts with *Select this text and delete* and then press ⃞Del⃞.

The instructional text is deleted.

25 Type **Please review this order and confirm your availability for delivery.** and then press ⃞Enter⃞.

The fax cover page is complete.

Save

26 On the Standard toolbar, click the **Save** button.

The **Save As** dialog box appears.

27 In the **File name** box, type FaxCover.

28 If necessary, click the **Save as type** down arrow and then click **Word Document**.

29 Navigate to the **SBS** folder on your hard disk, double-click the **Word** folder, double-click the **FormattingDoc folder and then click Save.**

The document based on the template is stored in the FormattingDoc folder.

Close

30 Click the **Close Window** button in the document window.

The FaxCover document closes.

Changing a Default File Location

W2002e-6-7

When you open and save a document or template, Word displays the **Open** or **Save As** dialog box with a default folder location. If you want to display a different default folder in the **Open** and **Save As** dialog boxes, you can change the location using the **File Locations** tab in the **Options** dialog box. The **File Locations** tab also defines where Word looks for files, such as clip art pictures files or Workgroup templates. **Workgroup templates** are templates shared over a network. If the **File Locations** tab doesn't display a file location for a file type, such as Workgroup templates, you can also define a location where you can easily find the documents and templates that you use most often.

To change the default file location of documents or templates:

1 On the **Tools** menu, click **Options**.

The **Options** dialog box appears.

2 Click the **File Locations** tab.

3 In the **File types** box, click a file type and then click **Modify**.

The **Modify Location** dialog box appears.

4 Navigate to the new default folder location and then click **OK**.

The **Modify Location** dialog box closes and the new default folder location appears in the **File types** box.

5 Click **OK** to close the **Options** dialog box.

Changing the Way Each Page Appears in a Document

W2002-3-1
W2002-3-3
W2002e-1-1
W2002e-2-1

Using a template is a great way to begin your document. Many of the documents that you create (with or without a template) will be more than a page or two. When you create a document that contains more than one page, Word paginates your document for you. To paginate a document means to insert page breaks-the page breaks that Word inserts are called **soft page breaks**. A soft page break appears as a dotted line across the page. If you don't like where Word inserts a page break, you can insert one yourself. A page break that you insert is called a **manual page break**. A manual page break appears as a dotted line across the page with the words *Page Break* in the middle. You insert a manual page break when you want to begin a new page.

tip

Word repaginates a document as you make changes to it. In other words, as you insert, delete and move text, Word changes where it inserts soft page breaks. Word does not change the location of manual page breaks; you must do that yourself.

Regardless of whether you keep Word's soft page breaks or insert your own manual page breaks, you should make sure that the page breaks do not leave widows and orphans. A **widow** is the last line of a paragraph printed by itself at the top of a page. An **orphan** is the first line of a paragraph printed by itself at the bottom of a page. Leaving a word or short phrase at the top or bottom of a page can interrupt the flow of long documents. To eliminate widows and orphans and to further control where Word inserts page breaks, you can use the options in the **Paragraph** dialog box. The following table explains the options in the **Paragraph** dialog box that you can use to specify how Word should treat situations that might cause paragraphs to break at undesirable places.

Line and page break options	
Widow/Orphan control	Prevents Word from printing the last line of a paragraph by itself at the top of a page (widow) or the first line of a paragraph by itself at the bottom of a page (orphan).
Keep lines together	Prevents a page break within a paragraph.
Keep with next	Prevents a page break between the selected paragraph and the following paragraph.
Page break before	Inserts a page break before the selected paragraph.

You have to apply the options in the dialog box on a paragraph-by-paragraph basis.

You can also insert a section break in your document. A **section break** identifies a portion of the document that you can format with unique page settings, such as different margins. A section break appears as a double-dotted line across the page with the words *Section Break* and the type of section break in the middle. There are several types of section breaks that you can insert. For example, if you want a section to begin on a new page, you insert a New page section break. You can also insert a Continuous section break or Even page or Odd page section breaks. Dividing a document into sections is especially helpful when you are creating long documents that cover a wide range of topics.

tip

As you make changes to your document, you might want to preview the way that it looks. Previewing your document helps you determine if and where you might need a manual page break or where you might want to insert a section break. To preview your document, click the **Print Preview** button on the Standard toolbar. Not only can you review the layout of your document in the Print Preview window, but you can also make changes to the layout from within the Print Preview window.

The way in which a page is laid out in a printed document is called the **page orientation**. The default page orientation in Word is portrait. When the page orientation is **portrait**, the page is taller than it is wide. **Landscape** orientation, on the other hand, is when the page is wider than it is tall. A document has only one page orientation unless you divide your document into sections. Then each section can have its own page orientation.

If you have a multiple-page document, you might want to insert page numbers. You can do this by using the **Page Numbers** command on the **Insert** menu. Page numbers appear in the lower- right corner of each page by default, but you can change their position and alignment by using the **Position and Alignment** options in the **Page Numbers** dialog box. You can change the position of the page numbers to the top and align them on the left or centre them, depending on your personal preference.

It is also possible to insert images into page headers.

You can also add information, such as the name of your company or the author of the document, that is printed on every page of your document. The **header** is text that is printed at the top of each page. The **footer** is text that is printed at the bottom of each page. To enter text for a header or footer, select the **Header and Footer** command on the **View** menu. When you select the command, the document view changes to Print Layout view, the Header section appears at the top of the page and the Footer section appears at the bottom of the page. The Header and Footer toolbar appears as well.

You can use the Header and Footer toolbar to enter document-related text, such as the name of the file or the date the document was last printed. If your document contains section breaks, you can have different headers and footers for each section.

The Garden Company often sends articles to its customers. An article written on composting needs to be paginated and the last page about the do's and don'ts of composting needs to be formatted differently from the rest of the article.

FormatPage

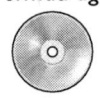

In this exercise, you insert page and section breaks, make sure that page breaks do not leave widows and orphans, change the page orientation and add a header and a footer in the document.

Open

1   On the Standard toolbar, click the **Open** button.

The **Open** dialog box appears.

2   Navigate to the **SBS** folder on your hard disk, double-click the **Word** folder, double- click the **FormattingDoc** folder and then double-click the **FormatPage** file.

The FormatPage document opens.

Print Preview

3   On the Standard toolbar, click the **Print Preview** button.

The Print Preview window appears.

Multiple Pages

4   Click the **Multiple Pages** button on the Print Preview toolbar and then drag the pointer to select four pages (2 x 2 Pages).

The Print Preview window shows the four pages of the document with a widow at the top of the second page.

5   On the **File** menu, click **Page Setup**.

The **Page Setup** dialog box appears, displaying the **Margins** tab.

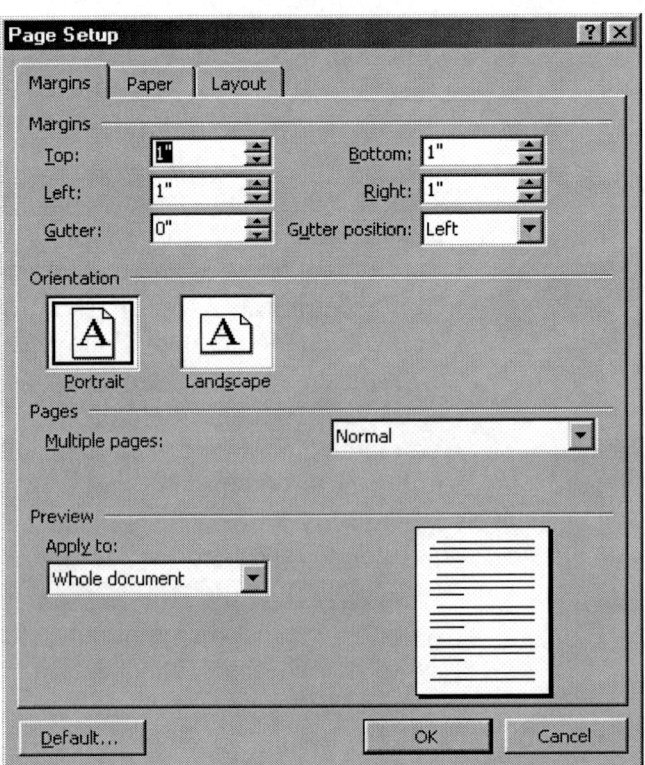

6   In the **Margins** area, select the value in the **Top** box and type **1.25"**, select the value in the **Bottom** box and type **1.25"** and then click **OK**.

The amount of blank space at the top and bottom of each page increases from 1 inch to 1.25 inches. The changes in the margins eliminated the widow at the top of page 2.

> ## tip
> The standard size of a page is 8.5 inches by 11 inches. With margins of 1.5 inches on each side, you are left with a work area that is 5.5 inches wide.

Close Preview
Close

7   On the Print Preview toolbar, click the **Close Preview** button to close the Print Preview window.

8   Press the ↓ key four times and then click in the first line of text in the paragraph that begins with the text *If you take the time.*

The first two lines of the paragraph appear at the bottom of page 2. You can keep these lines of text with the rest of the paragraph.

9   On the **Format** menu, click **Paragraph** to display the **Paragraph** dialog box and then click the **Line and Page Breaks** tab, if necessary.

10   If necessary, select the **Widow/Orphan control** check box, select the **Keep lines together** check box and then click **OK**.

The page break moves up so that all the lines of text in the paragraph appear on the same page.

11   Press ↓ twice and then click to the left of the text *Hot or Cold?.*

12   On the **Insert** menu, click **Break** to display the **Break** dialog box.

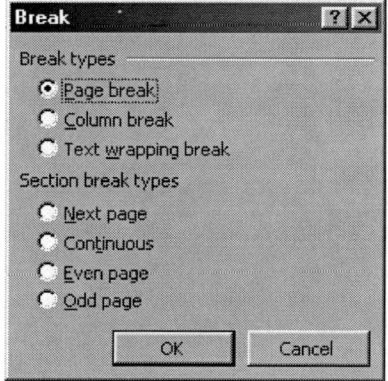

13   In the **Break types** area, verify that the **Page break** option is selected and then click **OK**.

A dotted line with the words *Page Break* appears, indicating that you inserted a manual page break. There are now five pages in the document.

14   Scroll down to the last paragraph and then position the insertion point to the left of the title *COMPOSTING DOs AND DON'Ts.*

15   On the **Insert** menu, click **Break** to open the **Break** dialog box, click the **Next page** option in the **Section break types** area and then click **OK**.

A double dotted line with the text *Section Break (Next Page)* appears.

16 Press `Ctrl` **+** `Home` to move the insertion point to the beginning of the document and then on the **View** menu, click **Header and Footer**.

The document is now in Print Layout view. At the top of the document window, there is an empty box in which you can enter the text for the header for section 1 of the document.

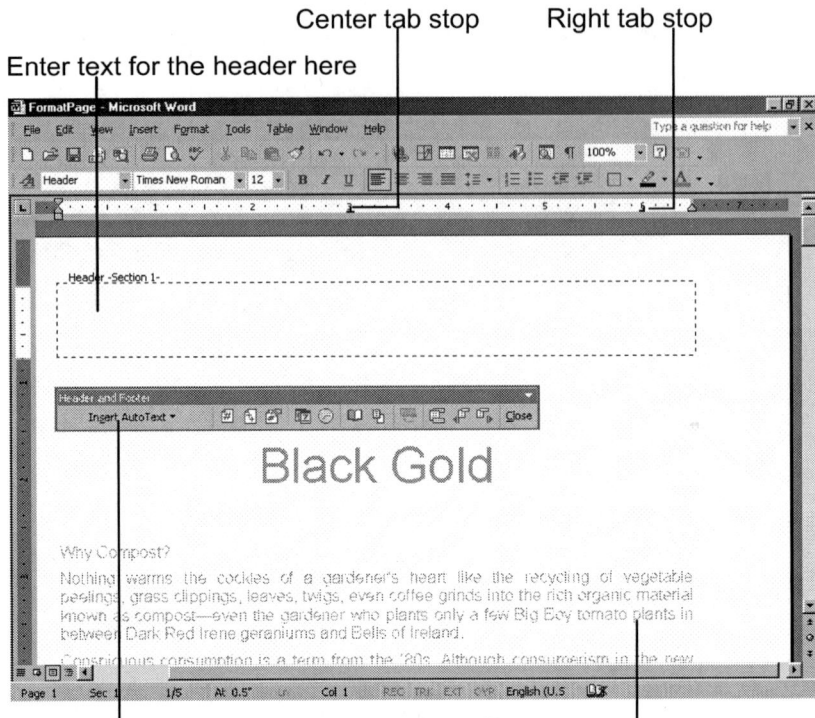

Center tab stop   Right tab stop

Enter text for the header here

Use to insert standardized text such as file name

Document text appears in the background

Show Next

17 Type **The Garden Company** and then click the **Show Next** button on the Header and Footer toolbar.

The insertion point is now in the **Header - Section 2** text box.

Same as Previous

18 On the Header and Footer toolbar, click the **Same As Previous** button, click the **Yes** button in the message box (if necessary), select the text *The Garden Company* and then press `Del`.

The company is deleted from the header so that it doesn't appear as the previous header.

Switch Between Header and Footer

19 Click the **Switch Between Header and Footer** button to switch to the footer text box. You do not want the same footer for section 2 as you have for section 1.

Same as Previous

20 On the Header and Footer toolbar, click the **Same As Previous** button and then click the **Show Previous** button on the Header and Footer toolbar.

The insertion point is now in the Footer - Section 1 text box.

Insert Page Number

21 Press the `Tab` key to move the insertion point to the center tab stop, click the **Insert Page Number** button on the Header and Footer toolbar and then click the **Close Header and Footer** button.

The first four pages in the first section of the document are numbered.

Print Preview

22 On the Standard toolbar, click the **Print Preview** button to display the Print Preview window.

Multiple Pages

23 On the Print Preview toolbar, click the **Multiple Pages** button, click and drag the pointer to select six pages (2 x 3 Pages) so that all five pages in the document are displayed and then click the last page in the document to enlarge the view of the page.

24 On the **File** menu, click **Page Setup** to open the **Page Setup** dialog box, click the **Margins** tab, click the **Landscape** icon, make sure that **This section** in the **Apply to** section is selected and then click **OK**.

25 Click the page with the pointer so that all five pages are redisplayed in the Print Preview window.

Note that the company name appears at the top of the first four pages of the document and that there are page numbers on the bottom of the first four pages. Note also that the last page is wider than it is tall and does not have header or footer text.

Close Preview

Close

26 On the Print Preview toolbar, click the **Close Preview** button to close the Print Preview window.

27 On the Standard toolbar, click the **Save** button to save the document.

Close

28 Click the **Close Window** button in the document window.

The FormatPage document closes.

Changing the Look of a Document with Styles

As you change the appearance of the text in your documents, you might find that you have created a look, or style, of your own. You may want to take advantage of the styles that Word provides. A **style** is a collection of text and paragraph formatting that you can apply to text throughout your document.

W2002-2-4
W2002e-2-2

You can apply a set of formatting changes to your documents at the same time using styles. **Character styles** format selected words and lines of text within a paragraph, whereas **paragraph styles** format entire paragraphs, including their indents, alignment and tabs. For example, a character style might be 18-point, bold, underlined and centred text, whereas a paragraph style might include a border and hanging indent. Instead of applying each of these formatting effects or attributes individually, you can apply all of theses attributes using a style.

Unless you choose a template from the **Templates** dialog box, the documents that you create use the same default template, the Normal template. In the Normal template (as in all templates), there are styles that make up the formatting attributes of the template. For example, the Normal style includes the default font style, font size and alignment. The default Normal style is 12-point Times New Roman text that is aligned on the left margin. The text that you type in your document uses the Normal style until you apply another style. For example, you might apply the Heading 1 style to text that you want to use as the title of your document.

Styles and Formatting task pane
new for OfficeXP

To apply another style to the text in your document, you can use the **Style** down arrow on the Formatting toolbar or the **Styles and Formatting** task pane. You can also create a new style. You can modify an existing style or create a new style based on text that you have formatted. When you modify a style, the text in your document associated with that style is updated to reflect the changes.

To enhance the appearance of the article on composting, The Garden Company wants to format the main headings by using styles.

FormatStyle

Open

In this exercise, you apply, modify and delete a style using the **Styles and Formatting** task pane.

1   On the Standard toolbar, click the **Open** button.

The **Open** dialog box appears.

2   Navigate to the **SBS** folder on your hard disk, double-click the **Word** folder, double- click the **FormattingDoc** folder and then double-click the **FormatStyle** file.

The FormatStyle document opens.

3   Select the line of text *Why Compost?*.

4   On the **Format** menu, click **Styles and Formatting**.

The **Styles and Formatting** task pane appears.

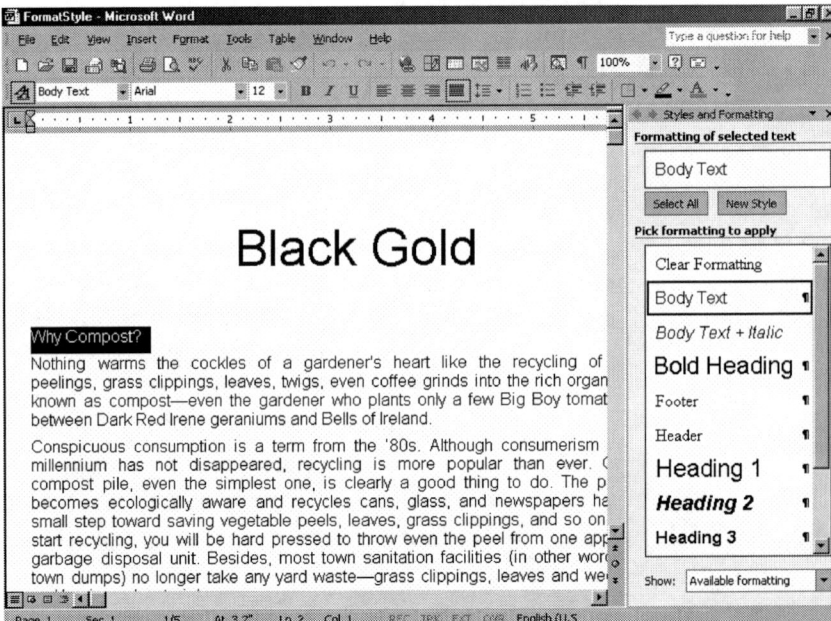

5   In the **Styles and Formatting** task pane, point to the preview box in the **Formatting of selected text** selection.

A ScreenTip appears, displaying the style and attributes of the selected text. In this case, the style is Body Text and the attributes are Normal style plus the default font Arial with the text justified and the spacing before and after the paragraph at 6 points.

6   In the **Styles and Formatting** task pane, scroll down the list and then click the **Heading 2** style in the **Pick formatting to apply** section.

The selected text changes to the Heading 2 style.

7   Click in the document, scroll down the document, hold down the Ctrl key, select the line of text *What Is a Compost Pile?,* scroll down the document, select the line of text *How Do You Make a Compost Pile?*, scroll down the document, select the line of text *Hot or Cold?* and then select the line of text *Compost and Soil.*

8   In the **Styles and Formatting** task pane, click the **Heading 2** style to apply the style to the selected text.

9   Scroll to the top of the document, click in the line of text *Why Compost?* and then click **Select All** in the **Styles and Formatting** task pane.

Word selects all the text in the document with the style of the selected text, which is Heading 2.

10   In the **Styles and Formatting** task pane, click **New Style**.

The **New Style** dialog box appears.

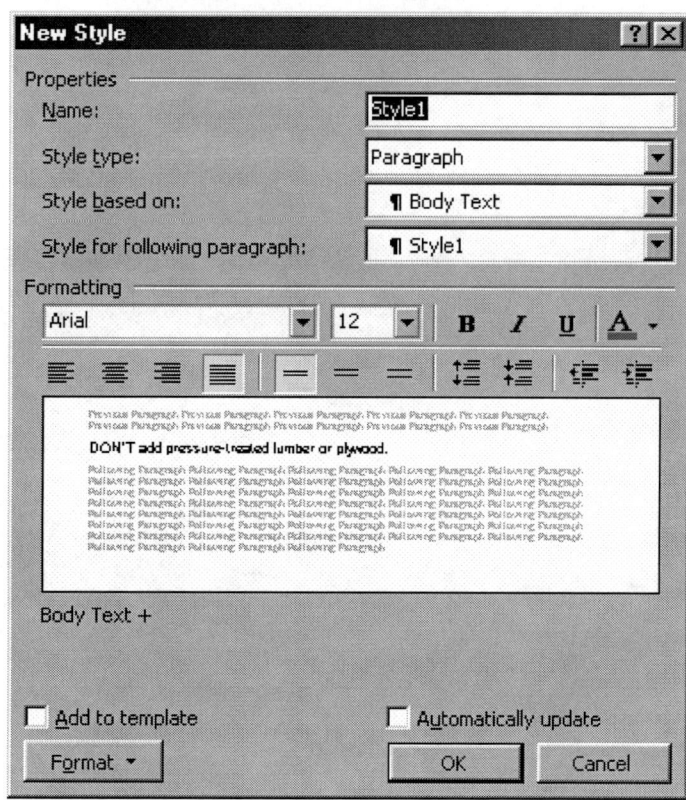

11   In the **Name** box, type **Heading 2 Plus** to create a new name for the style.

12   In the **Formatting** area, click the **Font Size** down arrow, click **16**, click the **Font Colour** down arrow, click the **Blue** colour box (sixth column, second row) and then click **OK**.

The Heading 2 Plus style appears in the **Styles and Formatting** task pane.

13   In the **Styles and Formatting** task pane, click the **Heading 2 Plus** style.

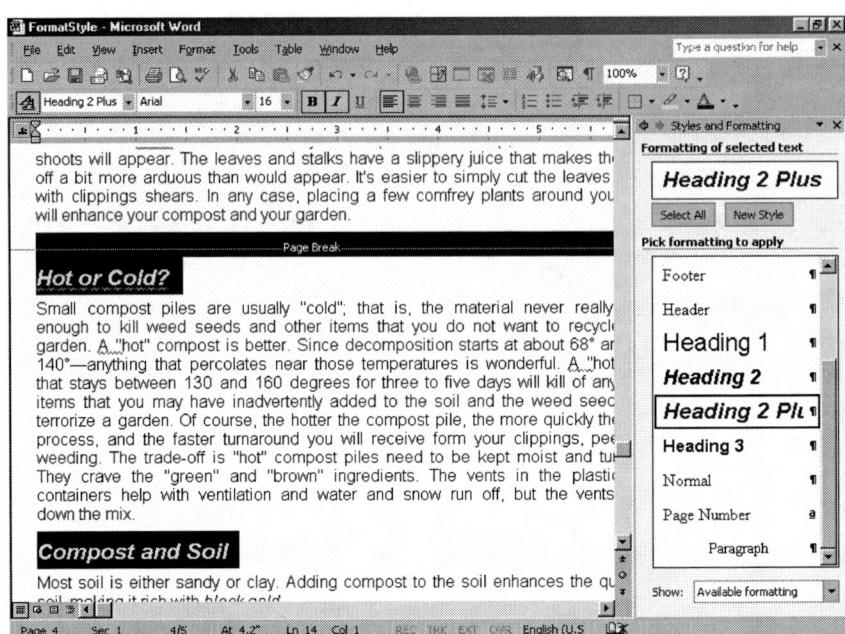

14   In the **Styles and Formatting** task pane, point to the **Heading 2 Plus** style, click the **Heading 2 Plus** down arrow on the right and then click **Modify**.

The **Modify Style** dialog box appears.

Italic

I

15   In the **Formatting** area, click the **Italic** button to deselect the attribute and then click **OK**.

The Heading 2 Plus style is updated along with all text with the style.

16   In the **Styles and Formatting** task pane, click **Heading 2**.

The selected text is formatted with the selected style.

tip

You can use the **Find and Replace** dialog box to search for a specific style and replace it with a different style. On the **Edit** menu, click **Replace**, click **More**, click **Format** and then click **Style**. In the **Find Style** dialog box, click the style that you want to find and then click **OK**. Click in the **Replace With** box, click **Format**, click **Style**, click the style that you want to use and then click **OK**. Click **Find Next** to search for the next occurrence of the style and then click **Replace**.

17   In the **Styles and Formatting** task pane, point to the **Heading 2 Plus** style, click the down arrow to the right and then click [Del].

An **alert** dialog box appears, asking whether you want to delete the style.

18   Click **Yes** to delete the Heading 2 Plus style.

19   In the **Styles and Formatting** task pane, click the **Show** down arrow and then click **Formatting in use**.

The styles used in the document appear in the task pane.

Close

20   20. In the **Styles and Formatting** task pane, click the **Close** button to close the task pane.

tip

If a wavy blue line appears under a word or phrase as you type, Word detects inconsistent formatting. To remove the wavy blue line and not correct the inconsistency, right-click the word or phrase and then click **Ignore Once** or **Ignore All**. To turn off the formatting options, on the **Tools** menu, click **Options**, click the **Edit** tab, clear **Keep track of formatting** check box and clear the **Mark formatting inconsistencies** check box.

21   On the Standard toolbar, click the **Save** button to save the document.

Close

22   Click the **Close Window** button in the document window.

The FormatStyle document closes.

Changing the Look of a Document with a Theme

You can change the entire look of a document by applying one of Word's 80 different themes. A **theme** is a unified look that incorporates the following: heading styles; text styles formatted with font effects, such as small caps and shading; lists with specially designed bullet characters; background colours; fill effects; and images. Each theme provides colour schemes and graphical design elements that project a special image or tone. For example, the Axis theme uses a background that looks like parchment paper and text design elements that match. You can use a theme when designing Web pages, reports and presentations.

FormatTheme

In this exercise, you apply a theme to an existing document and then display the theme styles in the **Styles and Formatting** task pane.

Open

1   On the Standard toolbar, click the **Open** button.

The **Open** dialog box appears.

2   Navigate to the **SBS** folder on your hard disk, double-click the **Word** folder, double-click the **FormattingDoc** folder and then double-click the **FormatTheme** file.

The FormatTheme document opens.

3   On the **Format** menu, click **Theme**.

The **Theme** dialog box appears.

4   In the **Choose a Theme** list, scroll down until the **Nature** theme appears and then click **Nature**.

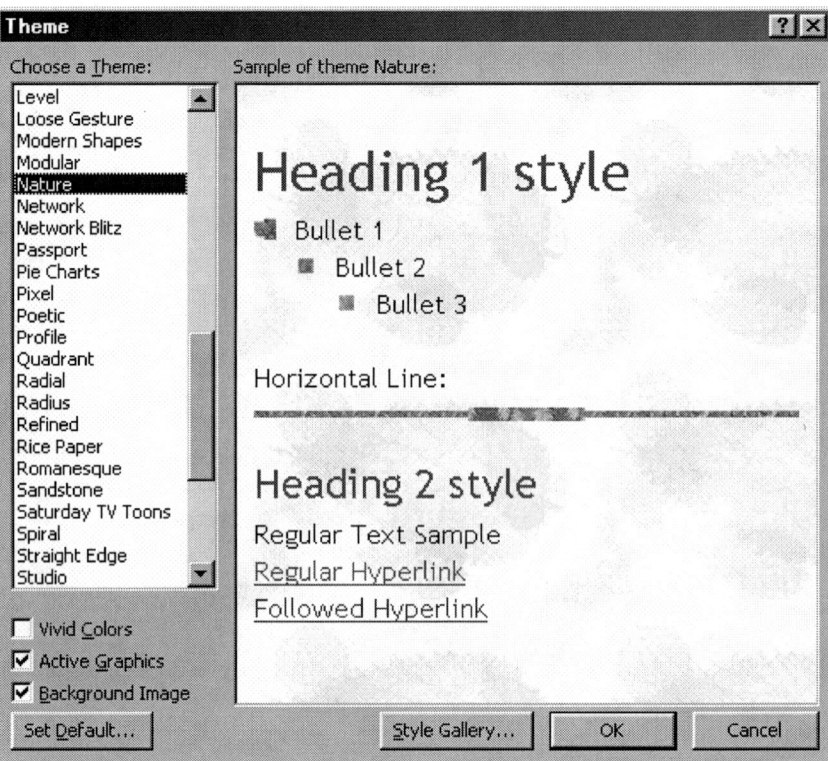

important

Some themes do not appear in the **Theme** dialog box until you install them from the Microsoft Office XP installation CD. To install a theme, click **Theme** on the **Format** menu, click a theme in the Choose **a Theme** list and then click **Install**.

5 Select the **Vivid Colours** check box to brighten the colours in the theme.

6 Click **OK**.

The Nature theme is applied to the document.

7 Select the line that starts with *Why Compost?*.

8 On the **Format** menu, click **Styles and Formatting**.

The **Styles and Formatting** task pane appears, displaying the styles used in the Nature theme.

Close

9 In the **Styles and Formatting** task pane, click the **Close** button to close the task pane.

10 On the Standard toolbar, click the **Save** button to save the document.

Close

11 Click the **Close Window** button in the document window.

The FormatTheme document closes.

Lesson Wrap-Up

To finish this lesson:

Close

1   On the **File** menu, click **Exit**, or click the **Close** button in the Word window.

Word closes.

Quick Quizzes

● How do you insert a page break?

● What is a section break?

● How do you insert page numbering?

● How do you add the file name to a header?

● What key do you use to move between the header and the footer?

● How do you create a new style?

● What is a theme?

● How do you insert a formula in a cell?

LESSON 4

Proof Reading and Printing a Document

After completing this lesson, you will be able to:

✔ *Check the spelling and grammar in a document.*

✔ *Preview and print a document.*

Before you share your documents with others, you should take a few steps to ensure that the documents are ready for distribution. One of the most important steps to take is to check the document's grammar and spelling to ensure that the words are spelled correctly and that the text is grammatically correct. You can use Word's spelling and grammar checker and thesaurus to correct spelling and grammar errors, add new words to Word's online dictionary and replace words with synonyms that improve readability and match the reading level of your audience. Because the online dictionary might not include specialized terms, proper names, or foreign words, you can use Word's AutoText feature to store and quickly insert these types of text. When you finish proof reading your document, you can preview the document to view and adjust the layout of your document before you print it. Then you're ready to print the document and any related materials, such as an envelope.

In this lesson, you'll proof read and print a letter for the assistant buyer at The Garden Company. You'll check the spelling and grammar in the Word document and then preview the document before you print it. You'll also create and insert an AutoText entry and print an envelope.

This lesson uses the practice files SpellCheck and PreviewPrint that you installed from this book's CD-ROM. For details about installing the practice files, see "Using the Book's CD-ROM" at the beginning of this book.

Checking the Spelling and Grammar in a Document

W2002-1-1
W2002-1-3

Proof reading a document involves checking the spelling of words, correcting grammatical errors and choosing language that best conveys your message to your audience. You should always proof read a document before you print and share it with others. Sending a document that is filled with spelling and grammatical errors creates a poor impression on your reader. You can use Word's Spelling and Grammar features to correct errors and maintain professional writing standards.

As you type the text of your document, by default Word underlines spelling and grammar errors with red or green wavy lines. A red wavy line indicates that Word does not recognize the spelling of the word; that is, the word is not included in Word's online dictionary. A green line indicates a possible grammar error. To fix individual spelling and grammar errors quickly, you can right-click a word underlined with a red or green wavy line to display a list of corrections from which you can choose.

In addition to correcting individual errors, you can check the entire document for spelling and grammar errors by clicking the Spelling and Grammar button on the Standard toolbar. When you start checking spelling and grammar, Word compares each word in the document with the words in its dictionary. Word stops at each red and green wavy line and displays an explanation of the possible error. For example, if a word is misspelled, the **Spelling and Grammar** dialog box identifies the misspelled word and provides a list of possible replacements. If Word finds a potential grammar error, the **Spelling and Grammar** dialog box identifies the problem and provides suggestions for correcting the error.

The options that are displayed in the **Spelling and Grammar** dialog box depend on the type of error that Word encounters. The following table describes the options in the **Spelling and Grammar** dialog box:

Button or Option	Function
Ignore Once	Leaves the highlighted error unchanged and finds the next spelling or grammar error. If you click in the document to edit it, this button changes to the Resume button. After you finish editing, click the **Resume** button to continue checking the spelling and grammar.
Ignore All or Ignore Rule	Leaves all occurrences of the highlighted spelling or grammar error unchanged throughout the document and continues to check the rest of the document. Word ignores the spelling or grammar of this word in this document and in all documents whose spelling is checked during the current Word session.
Next	Accepts manual changes in a document and continues to check the document.
Add to Dictionary	Adds the selected word in the Not in dictionary box to the custom dictionary. A custom dictionary contains words you have added.
Change	Changes the highlighted error to the word that you select in the Suggestions box.

Button or Option	Function
Change All	Changes all occurrences of the highlighted error to the word that you select in the Suggestions box and then continues to check the rest of the document.
Explain	Provides more information about the grammar error.
AutoCorrect	Adds the spelling error and its correction to the AutoCorrect list so that Word corrects it automatically as you type.
Undo	Undoes the last spelling or grammar action that you performed.
Options	Opens the **Spelling and Grammar Options** dialog box. Use this dialog box to open a different custom dictionary or to change the rules that Word uses to check spelling and grammar.

You can activate the **Show readability statistics** option from the **Spelling and Grammar** tab of the **Options** dialog box.

To make sure that you are using the exact words in your documents, you can use Word's thesaurus. For example, the language that you use in a letter to a friend is different from the language that you use in business correspondence. You can use the thesaurus to look up alternative words or synonyms for a selected word. To use the thesaurus, select the word that you want to look up, point to Language on the **Tools** menu and then click **Thesaurus**. The **Thesaurus** dialog box appears, displaying a list of synonyms with equivalent meanings.

Word you want to look up

Meanings

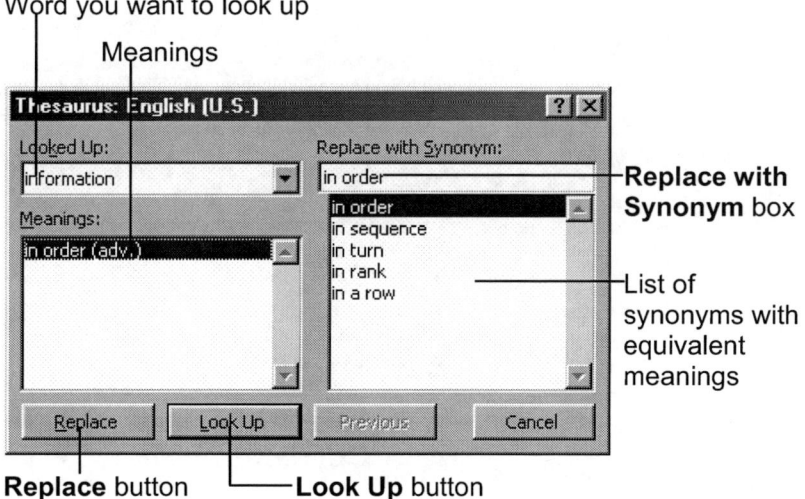

Replace with **Synonym** box

List of synonyms with equivalent meanings

Replace button   **Look Up** button

SpellCheck

In this exercise, you check the spelling in the document and add common terms that are not already in the online dictionary. You find, review and correct a grammar error and use the thesaurus to replace one word with another.

Open

1   Start Word, if necessary.

2   On the Standard toolbar, click the **Open** button.

The **Open** dialog box appears.

3   Navigate to the SBS folder on your hard disk, double-click the **Word** folder, double- click the **ProofingPrint** folder and then double-click the **SpellCheck** file.

The SpellCheck document opens, displaying red and green wavy lines.

Spelling and Grammar

4   On the Standard toolbar, click the **Spelling and Grammar** button.

The **Spelling and Grammar** dialog box appears, highlighting the first word that Word does not recognize. The online dictionary contains many common first and last names, but it does not recognize unusual or foreign names.

troubleshooting

If the spelling and grammar checker doesn't find the errors in this document, you need to reset the spelling and grammar checker. On the **Tools** menu, click **Options**, click the **Spelling & Grammar** tab, click **Recheck Document** and then click **Yes** to recheck words and grammar that were previously checked or that you chose to ignore.

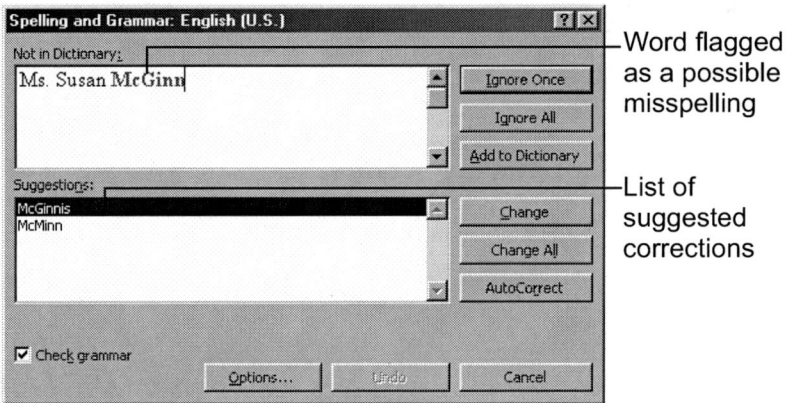

Word flagged as a possible misspelling

List of suggested corrections

5   Click **Ignore Once** to skip the name.

Word stops at the next word that it does not recognise - bot.

6   In the **Suggestions** box, click **both** and then click **Change**.

Word corrects the misspelling. The next flagged word is envrionmentally.

7   In the **Suggestions** box, click **environmentally** and then click **AutoCorrect** to redefine the AutoCorrect entry.

Word adds the correction to the AutoCorrect list. The next time that you type envrionmentally by mistake, Word will correct the spelling for you as you type.

Word flags harty as a possible misspelling.

8   With the word hearty selected in the **Suggestions** box, click **Change All** to change this and subsequent occurrences of harty to hearty.

Word corrects both misspellings and then flags crassula as a word that it doesn't recognize.

9   Click **Ignore All**.

Because this is the correct spelling of crassula, a type of plant, you can skip any other instances of crassula in the letter.

Word stops at the next word that it does not recognize-this time a Latin word.

10   Click **Add to Dictionary** three times to add to the custom dictionary the next three Latin words that Word does not recognize.

The three Latin words in italics are spelled correctly. By adding them to the custom dictionary, you prevent Word from flagging them later.

Word flags a possible grammar error in green and indicates that this text could be a sentence fragment. The sentence is missing a verb.

Grammar error highlighted in green

11   In the **Spelling and Grammar** dialog box, click before the word available in the highlighted text, type are, press [Space] and then click **Change**.

An alert message appears, indicating that Word has finished checking the spelling and grammar in the document.

12   Click **OK** to close the alert message.

13   Press [Ctrl] **+** [Home] to move the insertion point to the top of the document.

14   Double-click important near the end of the first paragraph to select the word.

15   On the **Tools** menu, point to Language and then click **Thesaurus**.

The **Thesaurus** dialog box appears, displaying a list of meanings associated with the word and suggested synonyms for important.

16   With significant selected in the **Replace with Synonym** box, click the **Replace** button.

Word replaces important with significant.

17 On the Standard toolbar, click the **Save** button to save the document.

Close

18 Click the **Close Window** button in the document window.

The SpellCheck document closes.

Translating Text in Another Language

Translate text
new for
OfficeXP

Word provides a basic multi-language dictionary and translation feature so that you can look up text in the dictionary of a different language, translate simple, short phrases and insert the translated text into your document directly from the Translate task pane. You can often use these translations to determine the main ideas in a document written in a foreign language. If you need to translate longer sections of text, you can connect to translation services on the World Wide Web directly from the Translate task pane. For important or sensitive documents, you might want to have a trained person do the translation, since computer translation might not preserve the text's full meaning, detail, or tone. You can also look up words or phrases in the dictionary of a different language, provided that the language dictionary is installed on your computer and enabled through Microsoft Office XP Language Settings. To enable a language, click the **Start** button on the taskbar, point to **Programs**, point to **Microsoft Office Tools**, click **Microsoft Office XP Language Settings**, click the **Enabled Languages** tab, select a language and then click **Add**.

To translate text in another language:

1 Select the text in your document that you want to translate.

2 On the **Tools** menu, point to **Language** and then click **Translate**.

The **Translate** task pane appears.

3 In the Translate task pane, click the **Current selection** option in the Translate what? section.

4 In the **Dictionary** box, select the languages that you want to translate from and to and then click **Go**.

The translated text appears in the **Results** box.

5 In the **Results** box, select the translated text and then click **Replace**.

The selected text in your document is replaced with the translated text.

Previewing and Printing a Document

W2002-3-5

Before printing a document, you should verify that its pages look the way that you want. You save time, money and paper by avoiding duplicate printing. Print Preview shows you exactly how your text will be placed on each page. This is especially helpful when you have a multi-page document. The Print Preview toolbar provides the tools that you need to check the presentation of each page. If you have headers and footers in your document, they also appear in Print Preview. You can change the layout of your document in Print Preview and you can even change the text.

Layout of printed document   Print Preview toolbar

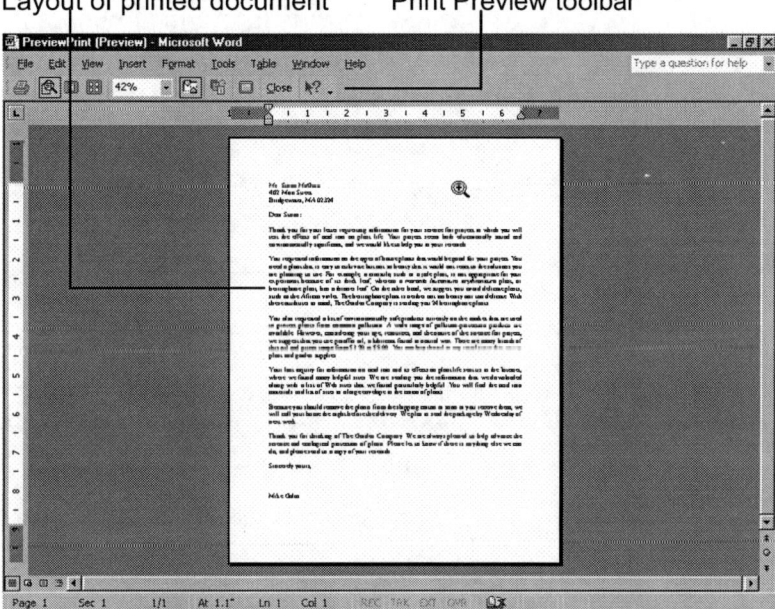

You can print your document by clicking the Print button on the Standard toolbar or the Print Preview toolbar. When you do, Word uses the current settings specified in the **Print** dialog box and prints to whichever printer has been set as the default. To open the **Print** dialog box to view or change print settings, on the **File** menu, click **Print**. In the **Print** dialog box, you can choose to print the current page or select certain pages that you want to print. You can also choose to print more than one copy of a document or print other document components, such as the list of comments or styles associated with the document.

You can print envelopes and labels using addresses that you have entered in a document. To do this, you select the lines of the address (or the text that you want for the label), point to Letters and Mailings on the **Tools** menu and then click **Envelopes and Labels** to open the **Envelopes and Labels** dialog box. You then choose the type of envelope or label that you need. You can also choose to print the envelope and label text in the font and font size that match those used in the document and you can include a return address on the envelope.

tip

To provide a return address, Word uses the personalized information that you entered when you installed Word. You can change that information on the User Information tab in the **Options** dialog box, which you open by clicking Options on the **Tools** menu.

An assistant at The Garden Company wants to preview a letter before printing it and adjust the layout of the letter, if necessary. He wants to print the letter on a printer other than the one he normally uses and needs to print an envelope for the letter.

PreviewPrint

In this exercise, you preview a document, adjust the top margin in the print preview window and select a new printer before sending the letter to be printed. After printing the document, you select the inside address and use it to print an envelope and label.

tip

To complete this exercise, you need a printer connected to your computer and the printer software installed.

Open

1   On the Standard toolbar, click the **Open** button.

The **Open** dialog box appears.

2   Navigate to the SBS folder on your hard disk, double-click the **Word** folder, double- click the **ProofingPrint** folder and then double-click the **PreviewPrint** file.

The PreviewPrint document opens.

troubleshooting

If an information icon appears in the document window, you can ignore it for now. Words and phrases underlined with dotted lines have a Smart Tag. Smart Tags provide options for using text as data in other programs. For example, you might want to add Susan McGinn's name and address to your Contacts list in Microsoft Outlook. To do so, click the **Smart Tag** and then select **Add to Contacts** from the list of Smart Tag options.

Print Preview

3   On the Standard toolbar, click the **Print Preview** button.

The letter appears in the print preview window, showing the entire page as it would appear on the printed page.

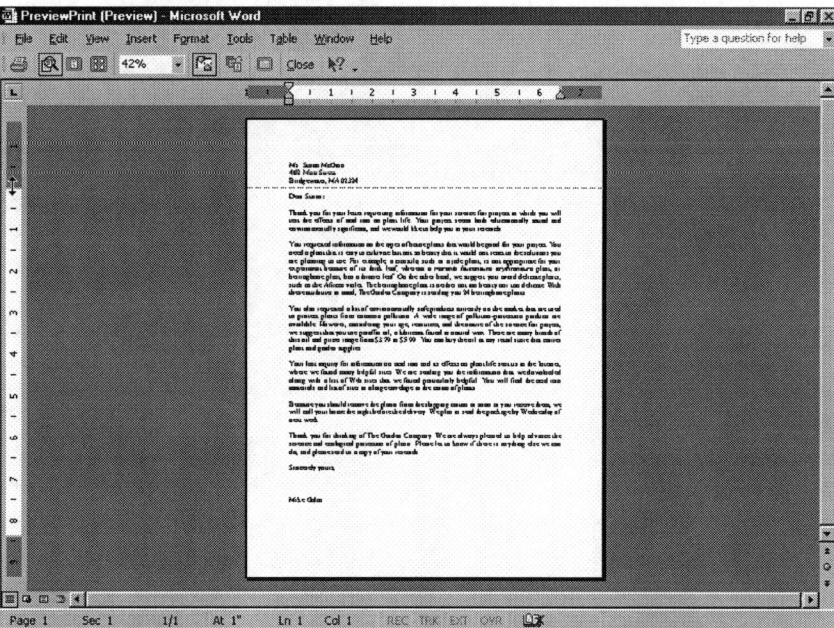

4   Position the pointer (which changes to the two-headed arrow) over the Top Margin indicator on the vertical ruler and then drag the pointer down about a half inch, making sure that the last line of text is not forced to another page, as shown in the illustration above.

Magnifying Glass (+)

5   Position the Magnifying Glass (+) pointer over the document and then click near the top of the document.

The document view zoom percentage changes to 100%, the actual size of the page.

Magnifying Glass (-)

6   Position the Magnifying Glass (-) pointer over the document and then click near the top of the document.

The zoom percentage is reduced.

Close Preview

7   On the Print Preview toolbar, click the **Close Preview** button.

The Print Preview window closes and the Word document window appears in Normal view.

tip

If you are satisfied with the current **Print** dialog box settings, you can click the **Print** button on the Standard toolbar to print directly without first viewing the settings.

8   On the **File** menu, click **Print**.

The **Print** dialog box appears.

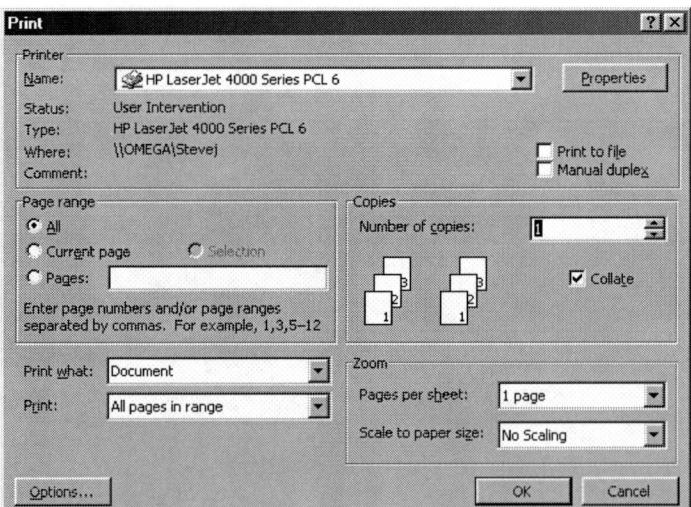

9   Click the **Name** down arrow, select a printer if necessary and then click **OK** to send the document to the printer.

10   Select the three lines of the inside address at the top of the document. (Do not select the blank line below the inside address.)

When you close the **Envelopes and Labels** dialog box, Word will ask you if you want to save the return address.

11   On the **Tools** menu, point to **Letters and Mailings** and then click **Envelopes and Labels**.

The **Envelopes and Labels** dialog box appears with the inside address selected in the **Delivery Address** box.

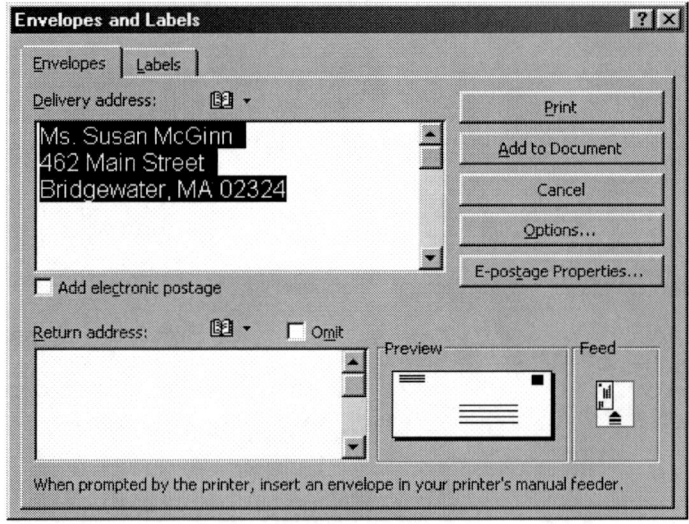

12   Select the **Omit** check box and then click **Options**.

This option excludes the return address when you print envelopes.

The **Envelope Options** dialog box appears, displaying envelope types and styles that your printer accepts. The default size is 10, which is acceptable.

13   Click **OK**, insert an envelope in the printer according to your printer manufacturer's directions and then click **Print**.

The envelope is printed.

14   On the **Tools** menu, point to **Letters and Mailings**, click **Envelopes and Labels** to display the **Envelopes and Labels** dialog box and then click the **Labels** tab.

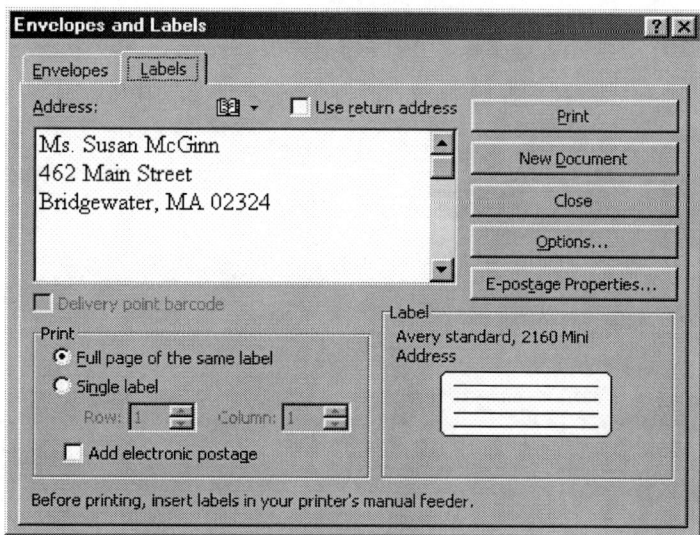

15 Click the **Single label** option.

Row 1 and Column 1 appear under the Single label option.

16 Click **Print**.

The label is printed.

17 On the Standard toolbar, click the **Save** button to save the document.

Close

18 Click the **Close** Window button in the document window.

The PreviewPrint document closes.

Lesson Wrap-Up

To finish this lesson:

Close

1 On the **File** menu, click **Exit**, or click the **Close** button in the Word window.

Word closes.

Quick Quizzes

● What is the Thesaurus?

● What does a wavy red line under a word mean?

● What does a wavy green line under a word mean?

● How to you check the spelling and grammar in a document?

● How do display a print preview of a document?

● How do you select print options?

● How do you print a document?

● How do you create envelopes and labels?

LESSON 5

Presenting Information in Tables and Columns

After completing this lesson, you will be able to:

✓ *Present and format text in a table.*

✓ *Present text in columns.*

You can use a table to group and organize the information in your document in a concise, consistent and easy-to-read format. A table organizes information neatly into rows and columns. The intersection of a row and column is called a cell. You can create a uniform table with standard-sized cells or draw a custom table with various-sized cells, or you can create a table from existing text. Once you create your table, you can enter text, numbers and graphics into cells. To help readers interpret the information in your table, you can arrange, or **sort**, the information in a logical order.

Once you have created a table, you can change the size of the table or of individual columns and rows. You can also insert and delete columns and rows as needed. To make the table visually appealing, you can format table text and add borders and shading to part or all of the table.

Tables often present numerical data. To perform standard mathematical calculations on numbers in a table, you can use the **Formula** command on the **Table** menu to add the numbers in a column or row, for example, or to find the average of the numbers. For more complex calculations, you can insert a Microsoft Excel worksheet into your document. Excel is a Microsoft Office program that you can use to perform complex calculations or statistical analysis.

Columns of text are another way that you can group and organize information in a document. Dividing text into columns is useful when you are creating a newsletter or brochure. In Word, you can define the number of columns that you want on a page. You can then choose to allow the text to flow from the bottom of one column to the top of the next column, as you see in newspapers. Or you can choose to end the column of text in a specific location, moving the subsequent text to the next column.

This lesson uses the practice files CreateTable, FormatTable and CreateColumn that you installed from this book's CD-ROM. For details about installing the practice files, see "Using the Book's CD-ROM" at the beginning of this book.

Presenting Text in a Table

W2002-3-4
W3003e-1-2
W2002e-3-2

It is possible to create a table around existing text. First select the text and then click the **Insert Table** button on the **Standard** toolbar.

To add a simple table to a document, you can use the **InsertTable** button on the Standard toolbar and then select the number of rows and columns you want from the menu that appears. If you want to set the size of the table along with other options, such as table formatting, you use the **Insert** command on the **Table** menu to open the **Insert Table** dialog box. You can also add a table by converting existing plain text to a table.

Once you create a table, you enter text or numbers into cells just as you would in a paragraph, except pressing the Tab key in a table moves the insertion point from cell to cell instead of indenting a paragraph. In addition to Tab, you can also use the arrow keys or the mouse pointer to move from cell to cell. The leftmost cell in a row is considered the first cell in the row. The first row in the table is good for column headings, whereas the leftmost column is good for row labels.

You can align text within a cell by selecting it and clicking the appropriate alignment button on the **Formatting** toolbar.

After you have created a table, you can modify its structure by inserting or deleting columns and rows. If the insertion point is positioned in the rightmost cell in the last row of the table, you can press Tab to quickly add another row to the bottom of the table. You can also use the **Table** menu to insert, delete and select rows and columns. To insert a row or column, you click to place the insertion point in the row or column where you want to insert one, point to **Insert** on the **Table** menu and then click **Rows Above**, **Rows Below**, **Columns to the Right**, or **Columns to the Left**. If you select more than one row or column and use one of the **Insert** commands, Word adds that number of rows or columns to the table.

Selection handle
newfor
OfficeXP

You can resize an entire table or each column or row individually to accommodate the text that you are presenting. To resize a table quickly, you can click and then drag the selection handle that appears in the lower-right corner of the table.

You can also merge cells to create cells of varying sizes. For example, if you want the title to be in the first row of your table, you can merge the cells in that row to create one cell that spans the table's width. If you need to divide a cell into smaller cells, you can split a cell into additional columns or rows. You can use the **Merge Cells** and **Split Cells** commands on the **Table** menu to combine or separate cells.

To change a table, you might need to select the entire table or specific rows or columns. The following table explains how to select part or all of a table.

To select	Action
A table	Click the **Select Table** button in the upper-left of the first cell in the table. Or on the **Table** menu, point to **Select** and then click **Table**.
A column or a row	Point to the first row in a column or the first column in a row and when the pointer changes to an arrow, click to select the column or row.
A cell	Double-click the cell.
Multiple cells	Click the first cell, hold down the [Shift] key and then press the [↓] or [→] key to select cells in a column or row, respectively.

tip

The document must be in Print Layout view before you can use the **Select Table** button and the selection handle.

To move a table in a document, you can click the **Select Table** button and drag the table to another location in the document. You can also use the **Cut** and **Paste** buttons on the Standard toolbar to move a table.

You will often create a table to accommodate multiple columns or lists of information. After you enter the text, you can sort the information in ascending or descending order and you can sort the information by column or row using the **Sort** command on the **Table** menu. For example, if you have a table with column headings for name, address and phone number, you can sort the table in alphabetical order by name to make it easier to find a person in the table.

The Garden Company needs to design an insert for its catalogue, *The Garden Company Herbs*. The owner of The Garden Company wants the insert to include three tables: an order form, a table of shipping and handling fees and a table of delivery services.

CreateTable

In this exercise, you create three tables. In the first table, you merge cells, enter text and add rows. To create the second table, you convert existing plain text to a table. Finally, you sort information in a third table.

1 Start Word, if necessary.

Open

2 On the Standard toolbar, click the **Open** button.

The **Open** dialog box appears.

3 Navigate to the **SBS** folder on your hard disk, double-click the **Word** folder, double- click the **AddingTables** folder and then double-click the **CreateTable** file.

The CreateTable document opens.

4 Press ⬇ to position the insertion point in the blank line below the *Please complete this form* sentence.

5 On the **Table** menu, point to **Insert** and then click **Table**.

The **InsertTable** dialog box appears.

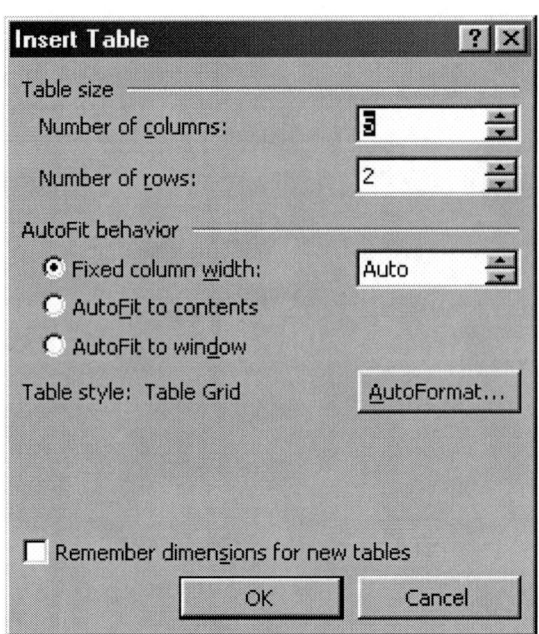

6 Make sure that the **Number of columns** box displays *5*, click the **Number of rows** up arrow to display *5* and then click **OK**.

A blank table with five columns and five rows appears. The insertion point appears in the first cell.

7 Position the pointer in the selection area to the left of the first row and then click to select the row.

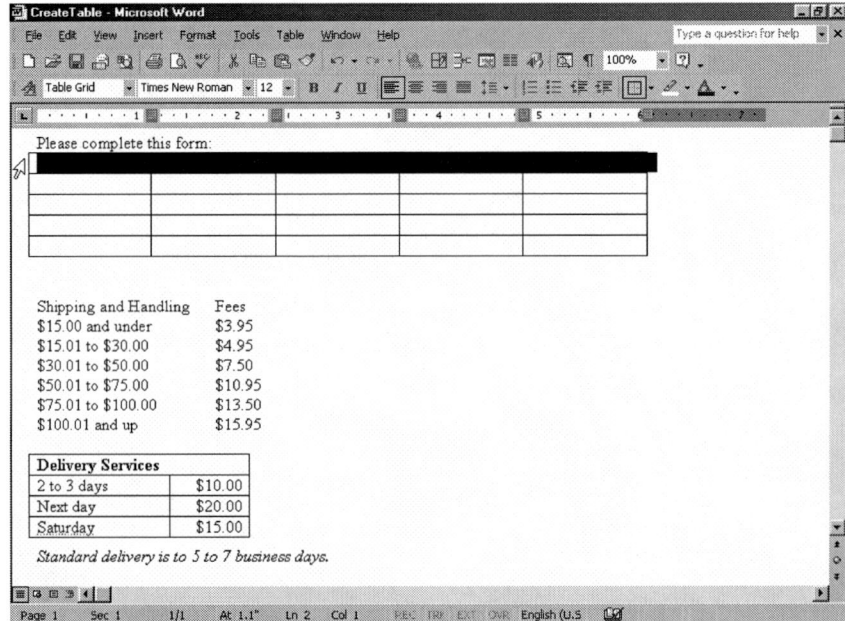

8 On the **Table** menu, click **Merge Cells** to combine the cells in the first row into one cell.

9 Type **The Garden Company Herb Plant Order Form**.

The text appears in the first row.

10   Click in the first cell in the second row and then type **Page No.**

11   Press [Tab] and type **Description**, press [Tab] and type **Quantity**, press [Tab] and type **Unit Price**, press [Tab] and type **Total** and then press [Tab] to move the insertion point to the first cell in the next row.

12   Type **25**, press [Tab] and type **Lemon Basil**, press [Tab] and type **3**, press Tab and type **2.29** and then press [Tab] and type **6.87**.

The text appears in the second row.

13   Position the pointer in the selection area to the left of the fourth row and then drag to select the last two rows.

14   On the **Table** menu, point to **Insert** and then click **Rows Below** to add two more rows to the table.

Two rows appear below the two selected rows.

15   In the last row, click in the first cell, hold down [Shift] and then press [→] four times to select the first four cells in the row.

16   On the **Table** menu, click **Merge Cells** to combine the cells in the first row into one cell.

17   Type **Total Order Amount** and then press [Tab] twice.

A new row is added to the bottom of the table. Note that the new row uses the structure of the preceding row.

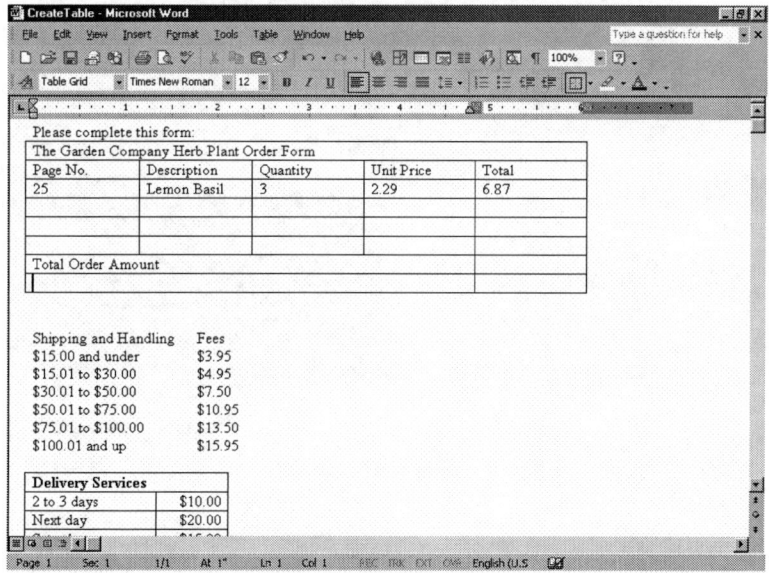

18   Type **Add Shipping and Handling Fee**, press [Tab] twice to add a new row and then type **Add Delivery Service Fee, if necessary**.

19   Press [Tab] twice to add a new row and then type **Total Amount Due**.

20   In the paragraphs below the table, select the block of text that begins *Shipping and Handling* and ends with *$15.95*.

21 On the **Table** menu, point to **Convert** and then click **Text to Table**.

The **ConvertText to Table** dialog box appears.

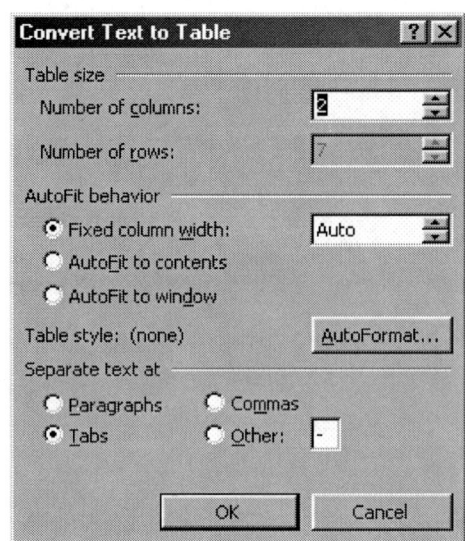

22 Make sure that the **Number of columns** box displays *2* and then click **OK**.

The selected text appears in a table with two columns and seven rows.

Resize pointer

23 Click in the table to deselect the cells, point to the right edge of the table until the pointer changes to a resize pointer and then double-click to resize the table to the width of the text in the cell.

24 Scroll down and then click anywhere in the Delivery Services table to place the insertion point.

25 On the **Table** menu, click **Sort**.

The **Sort** dialog box appears.

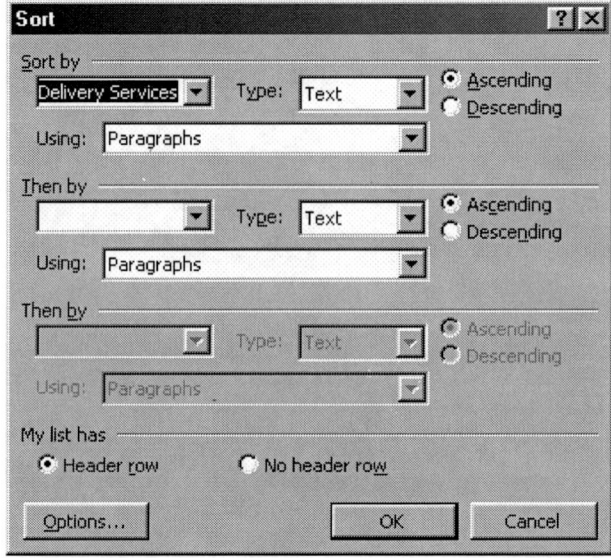

26 Click the **Sort by** down arrow, click **(Column2)** if necessary, click the **Descending** option, make sure the **Header row** option in the **My list has** area is selected and then click **OK** to sort the table in descending order by Column2.

Print Layout View

27 Click the **Print Layout View** button and then scroll down the document window to bring the Delivery Services table, the Shipping and Handling Fees table and the bottom of the Order Form table into view.

Select Table

28 Hold down the **Select Table** button in the upper-left corner of the Delivery Services table to select the table.

29 Drag the outline of the table up and to the right of the Shipping and Handling Fees table, aligning the top of the Delivery Services table with the top of the Shipping and Handling table and the right side of the Delivery Services table with the right side of the Order Form table.

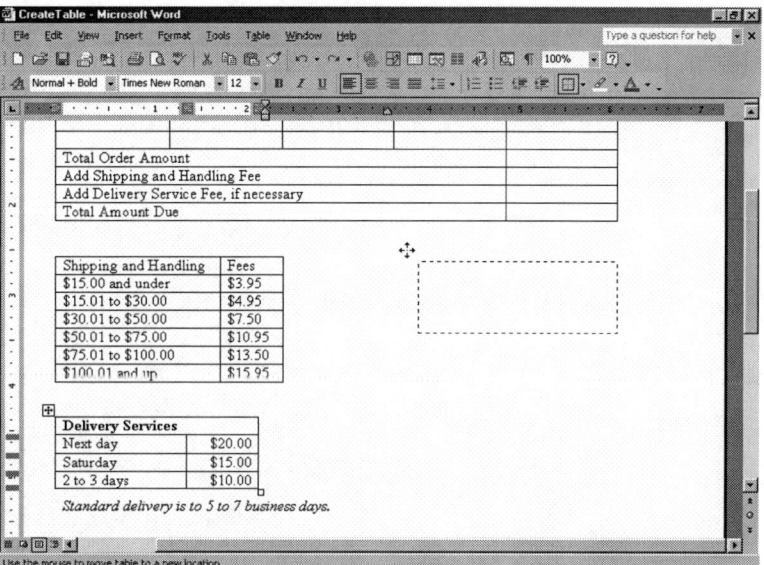

30 When the Delivery Services table is positioned correctly, release the mouse button.

31 Point to the Delivery Services table and then drag the selection handle in the lower-right corner down, releasing the mouse button when the lower edge of the Delivery Services table is aligned with the lower edge of the Shipping and Handling Fees table to align the tables.

32 On the Standard toolbar, click the **Save** button to save the document.

Close Window

33 Click the **Close Window** button in the document window.

The CreateTable document closes.

Formatting Text in a Table

To enhance the appearance of the text in a table, you can format it using the buttons on the Formatting toolbar, just as you would when formatting any text in a Word document. You can also format the structure of the table by adding borders and shading.

W2002-3-4

You can use the buttons on the Formatting toolbar to change the appearance and alignment of the text in a cell. To modify the table or cell borders, you use the **Borders and Shading** command on the **Format** menu, which opens the **Borders and Shading** dialog box. You can also add shading to the table or cells using the options on the **Shading** tab in the **Borders and Shading** dialog box.

Table styles new for **Office**XP

To format a table and its text quickly, you can apply a **Table AutoFormat** using the **Table AutoFormat** command on the **Table** menu. The **Table AutoFormat** dialog box provides 18 predesigned table formats that include a variety of borders, colours and attributes, such as italics, that will give your table a professional look. This is useful for quickly formatting a table. You can also create your own table style to quickly make one table look like another. Select a table, open the **Table AutoFormat** dialog box, click **New** or select a table style and click **Modify** and then use the formatting options to define the table style.

To make sure that the tables in The Garden Company's catalogue are easily distinguishable from one another but also complementary, the owner will format the tables.

FormatTable

In this exercise, you format the text in a table and add shading to a cell. You also apply an AutoFormat and add a border to a table.

1   On the Standard toolbar, click the **Open** button.

Open

The **Open** dialog box appears.

2   Navigate to the **SBS** folder on your hard disk, double-click the **Word** folder, double- click the **AddingTables** folder and then double-click the **FormatTable** file.

The FormatTable document opens.

troubleshooting

The document should open in Print Layout view. If the document is in Normal view, click the **Print Layout View** button.

3   Position the pointer in the selection area to the left of the first row in the Order Form table and then click to select the first row.

4   On the Formatting toolbar, click the **Font** down arrow and then click **Arial**. Click the **Font Size** down arrow and then click **16**.

The font style changes to Arial and the size changes to 16 points.

Center

5   On the Formatting toolbar, click the **Bold** button and then click the **Center** button.

The text appears in the centre of the cell with the bold formatting style.

6   On the **Format** menu, click **Borders and Shading**.

The **Borders and Shading** dialog box appears.

7   Click the **Shading** tab.

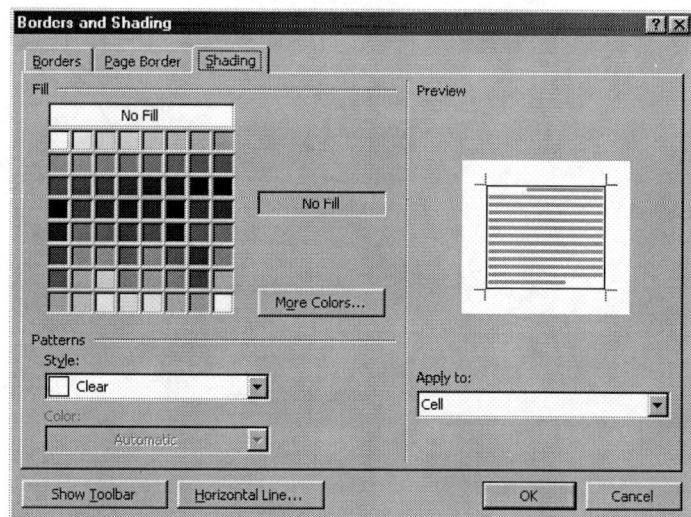

8 Click the **Light Yellow** colour box in the colour palette (last row, third column) and then click **OK**.

Word adds light yellow shading to the background of the first row.

9 Select the third row in the table.

Italic

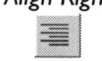

10 On the Formatting toolbar, click the **Italic** button to change the selected text to italic.

Font Colour

11 On the Formatting toolbar, click the **Font Colour** down arrow and then click the **Red** colour box in the colour palette (third row, first column) to change the selected text to red.

12 Select the last four rows in the Order Form table.

Align Right

13 On the Formatting toolbar, click the **Align Right** button.

Word aligns the text in the last four rows of the table along the right margin.

14 Click anywhere in the Shipping and Handling table to place the insertion point.

15 On the **Table** menu, click **Table AutoFormat**.

The **Table AutoFormat** dialog box appears.

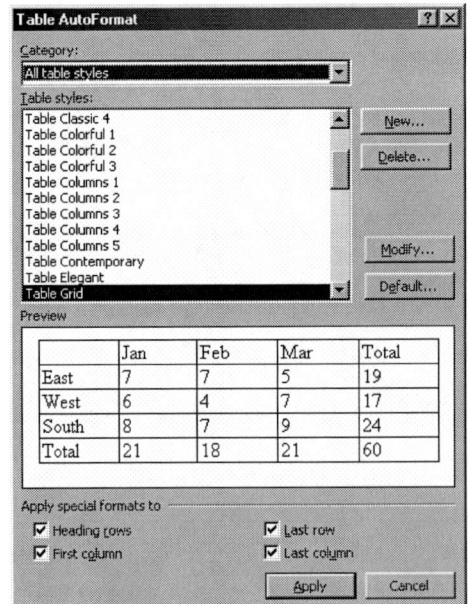

16 Scroll down the **Table styles** list, click **Table List8** and then click **Apply**.

The Shipping and Handling Fees table is formatted in contrasting colours with a dark border.

17 Click anywhere in the Delivery Services table to place the insertion point.

18 On the **Format** menu, click **Borders and Shading** to open the **Borders and Shading** dialog box and then click the **Borders** tab.

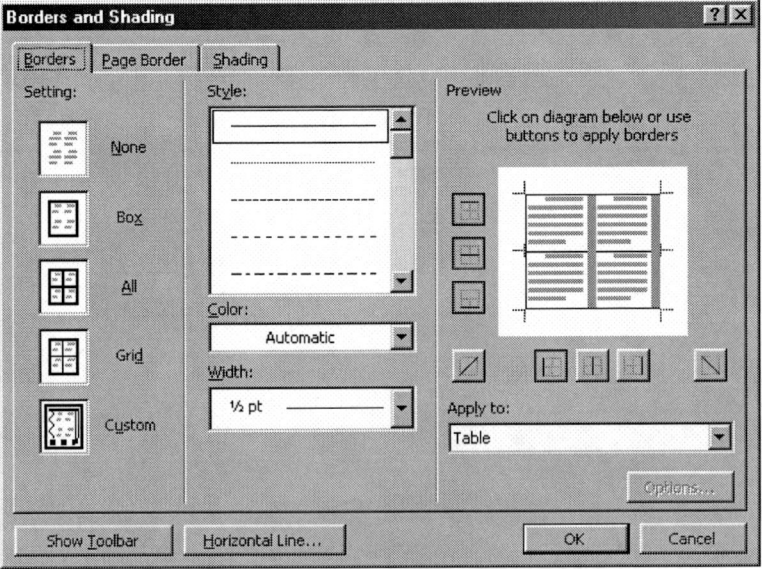

19 In the **Setting** area, click the **All** icon, if necessary, to select it.

20 In the **Style** list, click the down scroll arrow twice and then click the double line border style.

21 Click the **Colour** down arrow, click the **Red** colour box in the colour palette (third row, first column) and then click **OK**.

Word adds a red double border to the entire table.

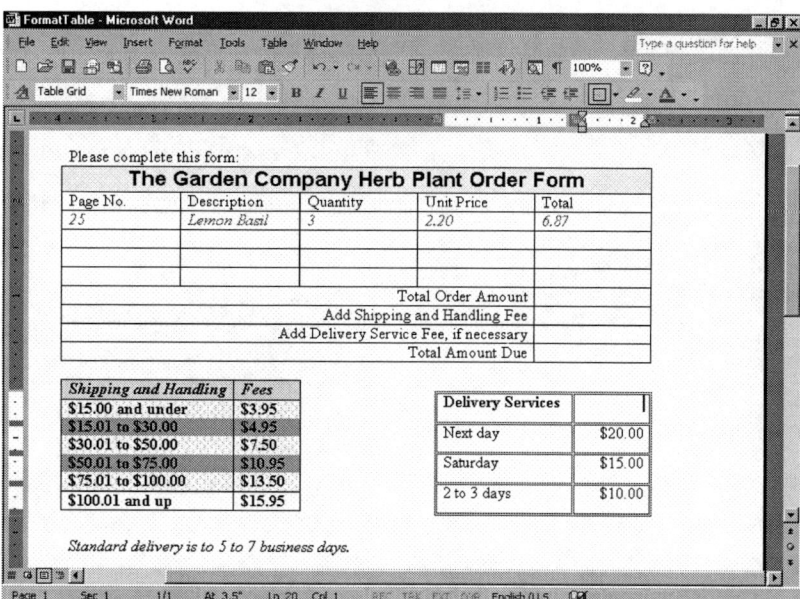

22 On the Standard toolbar, click the **Save** button to save the document.

Close Window

23 Click the **Close Window** button in the document window.

The FormatTable document closes.

Presenting Text in Columns

W2002-3-2

When you want to create a document, such as a newsletter, columns are a useful way to present information. In Word, a column is a block of text that has its own margins. You can divide a document into two, three, or more columns of text. (If you decide that you don't want to divide your document into multiple columns, you can format the document as one column--which is the default setting for any Word document.) When you divide a document into columns, the text flows, or snakes, from the top of one column to the top of the next. If you want the columns to be equal in length, you can insert a column break to force the text to move to the top of the next column.

After you break text into columns, you can change the width of a column. You can also format column text as you would any other text. For example, you can change the indentation or the alignment of text in a column using the horizontal ruler or the alignment buttons on the Formatting toolbar.

The owner of The Garden Company has written a nine-step procedure for cultivating an herb garden. The document must be set up in four columns to match other marketing materials.

CreateColumn

In this exercise, you format text into four columns and reduce the amount of space between the columns and indent column text. You also break the columns at specific locations rather than allowing the text to flow naturally from one column to the next.

Open

1 On the Standard toolbar, click the **Open** button.

The **Open** dialog box appears.

2   Navigate to the **SBS** folder on your hard disk, double-click the **Word** folder, double- click the **AddingTables** folder and then double-click the **CreateColumn** file.

The CreateColumn document opens.

3   On the **Format** menu, click **Columns**.

The **Columns** dialog box appears.

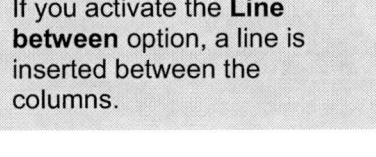

If you activate the **Line between** option, a line is inserted between the columns.

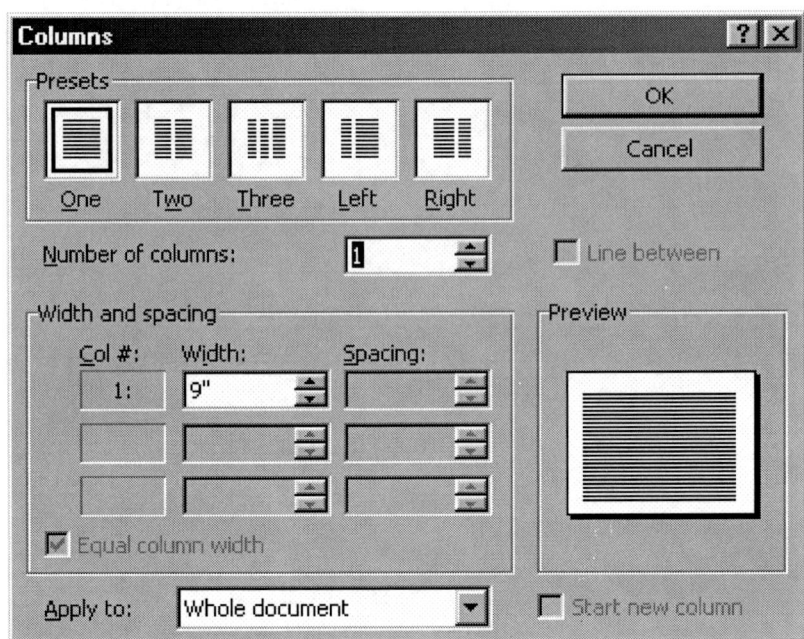

4   Click the **Number of columns** up arrow until **4** appears and then click **OK**.

The document view changes to Print Layout view and the document is divided into four columns.

5   On the **Edit** menu, click **Select All** to select all the text in the document.

6   On the Formatting toolbar, click the **Justify** button to align the text in the columns and then click in the document to deselect the text.

Justify

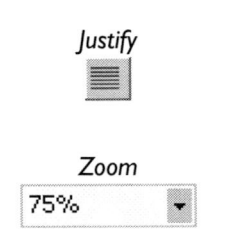

Zoom

75%

7   On the Standard toolbar, click the **Zoom** down arrow and then click **75%** so that more of the document is displayed in the document window.

Hanging Indent marker   **Right Margin** indicator

8   Point to the **Right Margin** indicator for the second column on the horizontal ruler. The pointer changes shape.

9   Click and drag the pointer 1/6 inch (one tick mark) to the right and then release the mouse button to resize the columns.

By dragging the pointer to the right, you decrease the spacing between the columns, which decreases the amount of white space on the page, visually enhancing the overall appearance of the layout of the document.

10   Click in the *NOTE* paragraph that appears after the *Step 2* paragraph.

11   Drag the **Hanging Indent** marker on the ruler 1/6 inch (one tick mark) to the right.

All lines except the first line of text in the *NOTE* paragraph are indented, which offsets this text from the step text.

12   Click in the *NOTE* paragraph that appears after the *Step 5* paragraph and then press the [F4] key to apply the same formatting to this paragraph.

13   Click to the left of the text *Step 5* to place the insertion point.

14   On the **Insert** menu, click **Break** to open the **Break** dialog box, click the **Column break** option and then click **OK**.

The text that appears after the column break moves to the top of the next column.

15   Click to the left of the text *Step 6* and then press [F4].

The Step 6 paragraph moves to the top of the fourth column. The columns are now more evenly divided across the page.

Print Preview   **16**   On the Standard toolbar, click the **Print Preview** button to view the document formatted in columns.

Close Preview

17 On the Print Preview toolbar, click the **Close Preview** button to close the print preview window.

18 On the Standard toolbar, click the **Save** button to save the document.

Close Window

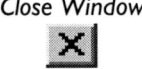

19 Click the **Close Window** button in the document window.

The CreateColumn document closes.

Lesson Wrap-Up

To finish this lesson:

Close Window

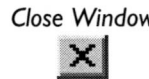

1 On the **File** menu, click **Exit**, or click the **Close** button in the Word window.

Word closes.

Quick Quizzes

● How do you create a table?

● How to you apply automatic formatting to a table?

● How do you remove a column?

● How do you select an entire table?

● How do you insert a row?

● How do you present text in a table?

LESSON 6

Working with Graphics

After completing this lesson, you will be able to:

✓ *Create a diagram.*

✓ *Insert and modify pictures.*

✓ *Create WordArt.*

You can insert and modify graphics in Word to make your documents more visually appealing and to convey information that is difficult to provide in textual form. A **graphic** is a picture or a drawing object. You can use the options on the Drawing toolbar to insert pictures and draw numerous objects without leaving Word. A **picture** is a photograph, a scanned picture, a bitmap, or clip art that was created outside of Word. Drawing objects are created within Word and include AutoShapes, diagrams, curves, lines and WordArt drawing objects. After you add a graphic to a document, you can enhance it with a variety of colours and special effects. You can also change the position of graphics in a document by using various layout options and changing how the text and graphics work together on the page.

In this lesson, you'll create a diagram to communicate information visually and relationally, insert pictures, change a picture to appear faintly in the background, change how text and graphics are laid out, insert WordArt and draw and modify shapes.

This lesson uses the practice files OrgChart, InsertPics Gardenco and WordArt that you installed from this book's CD-ROM. For details about installing the practice files, see "Using the Book's CD-ROM" at the beginning of this book.

Creating a Diagram

W2002-5-2

Diagram
new for
OfficeXP

To help you organize personnel data or other types of information, you can insert and modify diagrams in your documents. A **diagram** is a visual and relational representation of information. A common diagram is an organization chart. You can also create cycle diagrams, radial diagrams, pyramid diagrams, Venn diagrams and target diagrams.

When you insert an organization chart into a document, the chart has placeholder text that you click and replace with your own. The boxes and the lines of the organization chart are objects that you can move and change.

OrgChart

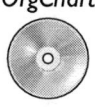

In this exercise, you insert and modify an organization chart.

1   Start Word, if necessary.

2   On the Standard toolbar, click the **Open** button.

Open

The **Open** dialog box appears.

3 Navigate to the **SBS** folder on your hard disk, double-click the **Word** folder, double- click the **Drawing** folder and then double-click the **OrgChart** file.

The OrgChart document opens.

4 Press ⌈Ctrl⌉ **+** ⌈End⌉ to place the insertion point at the end of the document.

Insert Diagram or Organization Chart

5 On the Drawing toolbar, click the **Insert Diagram or Organization Chart** button.

tip

If the Drawing toolbar is not open on your screen, on the **View** menu, point to **Toolbars** and then click **Drawing**.

The **Diagram Gallery** dialog box appears, with the Organization Chart selected by default.

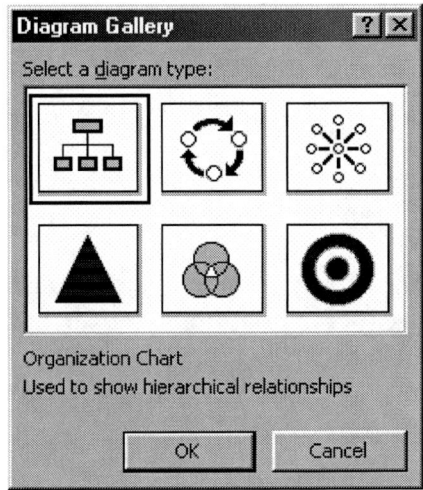

6 Click **OK**.

An organization chart is inserted into the document and the Organization Chart toolbar appears.

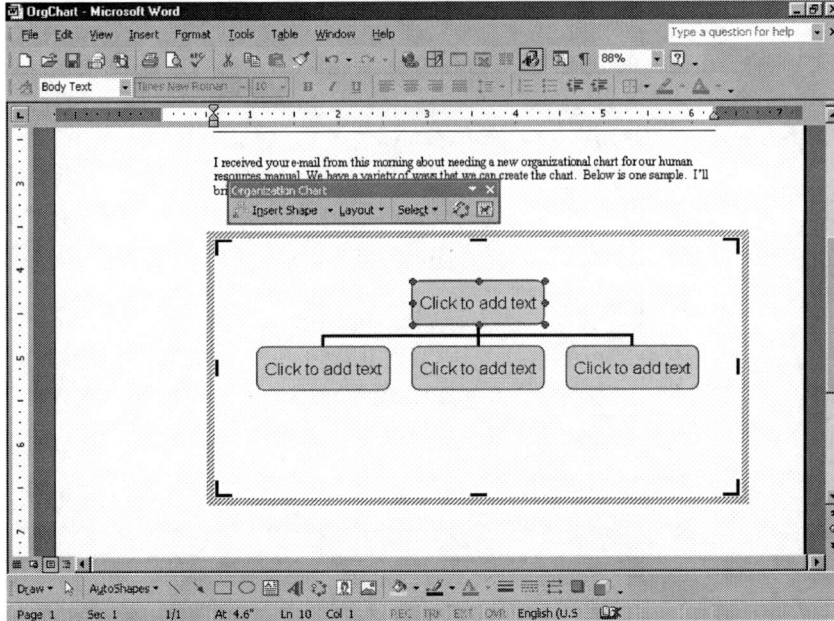

7   In the organization chart, click the top box to place the insertion point and then type **Catherine Turner**.

8   Click the first box in the second row, type **Kim Yoshida**, click the second box in the second row, type **Mike Galos**, click the third box in the second row and then type **David Campbell**.

All boxes contain names. The last box is still selected.

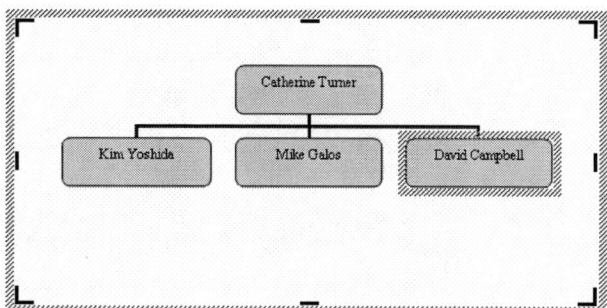

9   On the Organization Chart toolbar, click the **Select** down arrow and then click **All Connecting Lines**.

All connecting lines in the organization chart are selected.

10   On the **Format** menu, click **AutoShape**.

The **Format AutoShape** dialog box appears.

11   In the **Line** area, click the **Colour** down arrow and then click the **Red** colour box (row 3, column 1).

The line colour selection is now red.

12   In the **Arrows** area, click the **Begin style** down arrow, click the second option in the first row and then click **OK**.

The lines in the organization chart are now red with arrows attached.

Autoformat

tip

You can quickly format an organization chart using a predefined style by clicking the **Autoformat** button on the Organization Chart toolbar.

13   Click a blank area of the document to deselect the organization chart.

14   On the Standard toolbar, click the **Save** button to save the document.

Close

15   Click the **Close Window** button in the document window.

The OrgChart document closes.

Inserting and Modifying Pictures

You can insert nearly any picture, scanned photograph, photo, or artwork from a CD-ROM or other program into a document in Word. When you use the **Picture** submenu on the **Insert** menu, you specify the source of the picture-a file, Word's clip art collection, or a scanner.

To insert a picture from a file on your hard disk, removable disk, or network, you use the **From File** command on the **Picture** submenu. To insert a picture from the clip art collection that comes with Word, you click the **Clip Art** command on the **Picture** submenu or click the **Insert Clip Art** button on the Drawing toolbar, which opens the **Insert Clip Art** task pane. Microsoft Office XP provides hundreds of professionally designed pieces of clip art that you can use in your documents. For example, you can insert clip art pictures of scenic backgrounds, maps, buildings, or people. If you have a scanner connected to the computer that you are using, you can scan and insert a picture using the **From Scanner** command. Once you insert clip art or any picture into your document, you can modify it by using the Picture toolbar.

The following table describes the buttons on the Picture toolbar:

Button Name	Button	Description
Insert Picture		Allows you to insert a picture
Colour		Allows you to change the colouring of the picture
More Contrast		Applies more contrast
Less Contrast		Reduces contrast
More Brightness		Applies more brightness
Less Brightness		Reduces brightness
Crop		Crops the picture
Rotate Left		Rotates the picture to the left
Line Style		Allows you to change the line style
Compress Pictures		Enables you to reduce the size of pictures
Text Wrapping		Allows you to wrap text around a picture
Format Picture		Allows you to change features such as colours, size and lines
Set Transparent Colour		Allows you to make selected colours in the picture see-through

Button Name	Button	Description
Reset Picture		Resets the picture to its original state

Watermarks
new for
OfficeXP

Watermarks are dimmed pictures or text that appear faintly in the background of your printed document. You can use a picture such as a company logo as a watermark, or you can use words such as *ASAP*, *CONFIDENTIAL*, or *DRAFT*.

The head buyer at The Garden Company wants to send a memo that contains a sample organization chart. She will insert clip art to enhance the chart and a watermark to indicate that the memo is confidential.

InsertPics Gardenco

In this exercise, you insert and modify clip art and then insert a watermark.

1 On the Standard toolbar, click the **Open** button.

The **Open** dialog box appears.

Open

2 Navigate to the **SBS** folder on your hard disk, double-click the **Word** folder, double- click the **Drawing** folder and then double-click the **InsertPics** file.

The InsertPics document opens, showing the insertion point to the left of the text *Memorandum*.

3 Press the Enter key and then press the ↑ key to place the insertion point in a blank line at the beginning of the document.

4 On the **Insert** menu, point to **Picture** and then click **From File**.

The **Insert Picture** dialog box appears.

Insert Picture

tip
You can also click the **Insert Picture** button on the Drawing toolbar to open the **Insert Picture** dialog box.

5 Navigate to the **SBS** folder on your hard disk, double-click the **Word** folder, double- click the **Drawing** folder and then double-click the **Gardenco** file.

The picture is inserted into the document.

6 Click The Garden Company logo to select it.

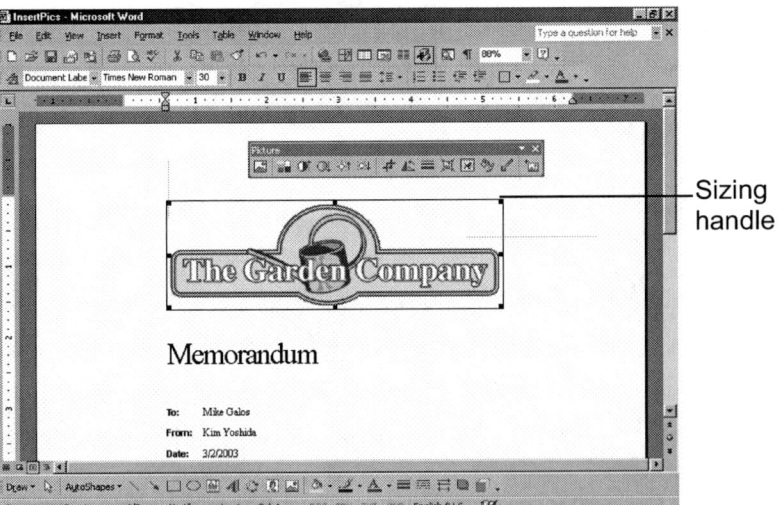

Sizing handle

To cancel a picture, click it and then press ☐ Del ☐.

tip
If the Picture toolbar is not open on your screen, on the **View** menu, point to **Toolbars** and then click **Picture**.

7 Drag the lower-right-corner sizing handle (which changes to a diagonal double-arrow) up and to the left until you reach the 4-inch mark on the ruler to resize the picture.

Colour

8 On the Picture toolbar, click the **Colour** button and then click **Washout**.

The picture is now washed out.

Less Brightness

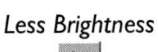

9 On the Picture toolbar, click the **Less Brightness** button four times to reduce the brightness of the picture.

More Contrast

10 On the Picture toolbar, click the **More Contrast** button two times to sharpen the picture.

11 Scroll down the document to display the organization chart.

Insert Clip Art

12 On the Drawing toolbar, click the **Insert ClipArt** button.

The **Insert Clip Art** task pane opens.

13 In the **Insert Clip Art** task pane, type **plant** in the **Search text** box and then click **Search**.

The task pane displays graphics associated with the keyword *plant*.

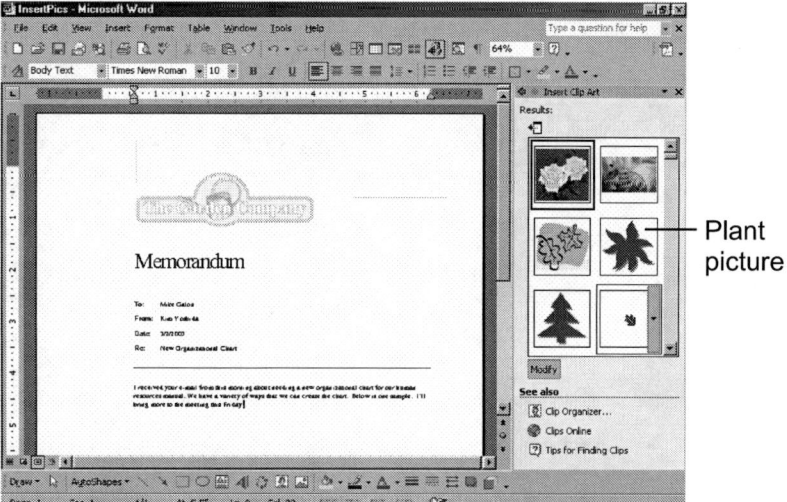

You can open the Microsoft Clip Organizer by selecting **Insert Clip Art** from the **Task Pane**.

Plant picture

14   In the **Results** area, click the plant picture and then click **Close** to close the **Insert Clip Art** task pane.

The picture is inserted into the document.

15   Click the plant picture to select it, point to the lower-right circular handle until the pointer changes to a double arrow and then drag up and to the left until the picture is about 1 inch by 1 inch in size.

The picture appears smaller.

16   Point to the plant picture until the pointer changes to the four-headed arrow and then drag the picture to the left of the Catherine Turner box in the organization chart.

The picture appears in the organization chart and the Organization Chart toolbar appears.

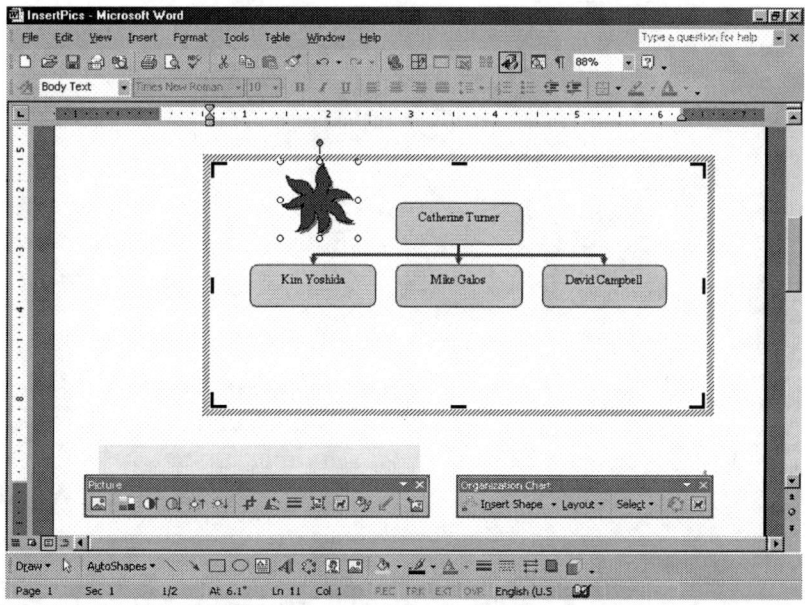

tip

If the Drawing and Organization Chart toolbars are blocking your view of the document, drag their title bars to move them out of the way.

17   Hold down Ctrl , click the plant picture and then drag it to the right of the Catherine Turner box to copy it there.

18 Click outside of the drawing canvas to deselect it.

19 On the **Format** menu, point to **Background** and then click **Printed Watermark.**

The **Printed Watermark** dialog box appears.

20 Click the **Text watermark** option, click the **Text** down arrow and then click **CONFIDENTIAL** to select a watermark style.

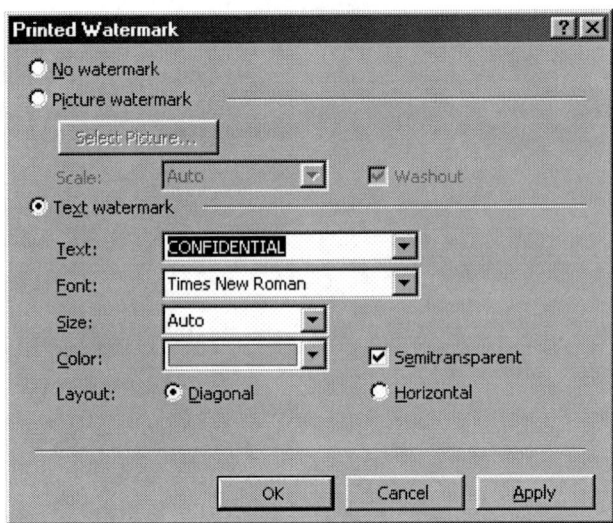

21 Click **OK**.

A *CONFIDENTIAL* watermark now appears faintly in the background at an angle.

22 On the Standard toolbar, click the **Save** button to save the document.

Close

23 Click the **Close Window** button in the document window.

The InsertPics document closes.

Creating WordArt

W2002-5-1

WordArt allows you to change the shape and appearance of text in your document. Use WordArt to create special effects for your text. You can make WordArt text appear curved, outlined, shadowed, or three-dimensional.

WordArt objects can be edited and default settings can also be changed, for example, changing the fill colour.

To create WordArt out of existing text in your document, select the text that you want to enhance, click the **Insert WordArt** button on the Drawing toolbar, click a selection in the **WordArt Gallery** dialog box and then click **OK**. The **Edit WordArt Text** dialog box appears with your text selection highlighted.

When you work with WordArt, you can use the WordArt toolbar, which opens when you insert or select a WordArt object. The following table lists the WordArt toolbar buttons and a brief description of each.

Button Name	Button	Description
Insert WordArt		Inserts WordArt
Edit Text	Edit Te_xt...	Edits text within WordArt
WordArt Gallery		Provides graphical options for your WordArt
Format WordArt		Allows you to change the colour, size and layout of the WordArt
WordArt Shape	Abc	Changes the shape of the WordArt
Text Wrapping		Changes the text wrapping around your WordArt
WordArt Same Letter Heights	Aa	Makes the letters in the WordArt the same height
WordArt Vertical Text	Ab b↲	Changes the alignment of the text from horizontal to vertical
WordArt Alignment		Changes the alignment of the WordArt
WordArt Character Spacing	AV↔	Changes the spacing between characters in the WordArt

The head buyer of the Garden Company is throwing a surprise birthday party for the owner. She is preparing a flyer about the party, which she will distribute to all The Garden Company employees.

WordArt

In this exercise, you insert and modify WordArt.

1   On the Standard toolbar, click the **Open** button.

Open

The **Open** dialog box appears.

2   Navigate to the **SBS** folder on your hard disk, double-click the **Word** folder, double- click the **Drawing** folder and then double-click the **WordArt** file.

The WordArt document opens.

3   Press the ↓ key twice to move the insertion point to the third line of the document.

Insert WordArt

4   On the Drawing toolbar, click the **Insert WordArt** button.

The **WordArt Gallery** dialog box appears.

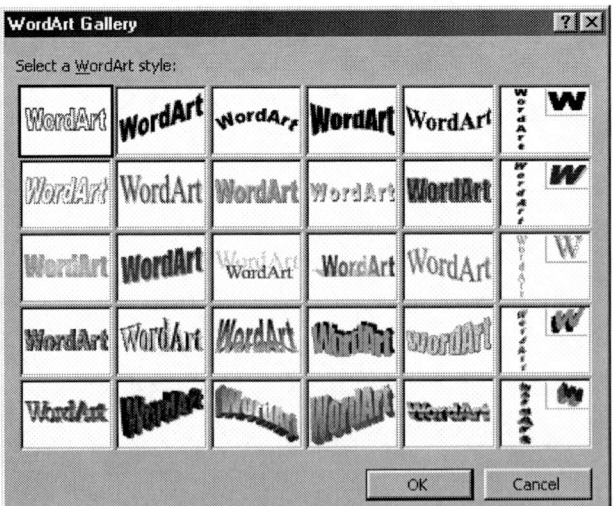

tip

If the Drawing toolbar is not open on your screen, on the **View** menu, point to **Toolbars** and then click **Drawing**.

5 Click the WordArt style in row 3, column 1 and then click **OK**.

The **Edit WordArt Text** dialog box appears, displaying *Your Text Here* as a placeholder.

6 Type **Special Guest: Her Mother!**. Click the **Size** down arrow, click **44**, click the **Bold** button and then click **OK**.

The text is inserted as an object.

7 Click the WordArt object to select it.

The WordArt toolbar appears and sizing handles surround the object.

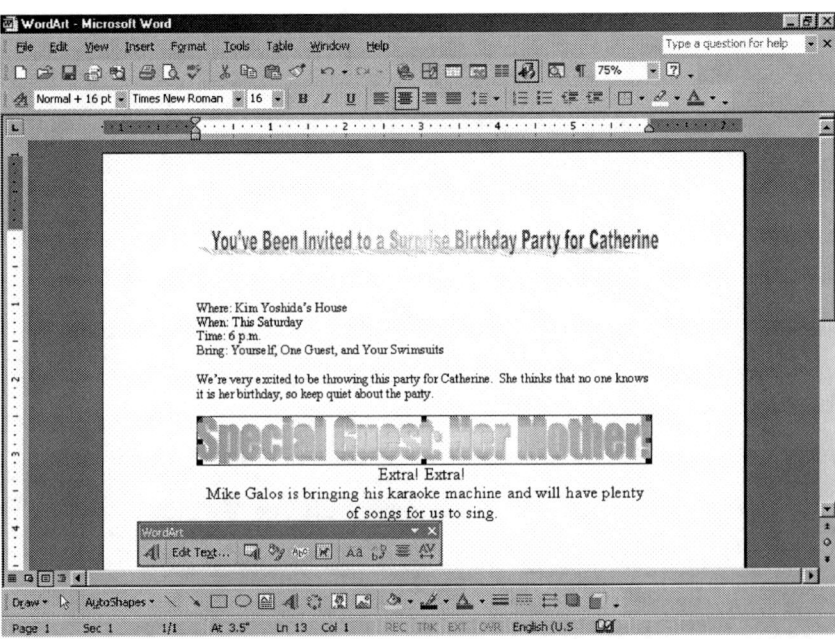

8 Drag the **WordArt object** down so that it appears above the text *Extra! Extra!*, as shown in the illustration above.

WordArt Character Spacing

9 On the WordArt toolbar, click the **WordArt Character Spacing** button and then click **Very Loose**.

The spacing between the letters in the WordArt increases.

WordArt Shape

10 On the WordArt toolbar, click the **WordArt Shape** button and then click **Arch Up (Curve)** on the submenu (row 2, column 1).

The WordArt shape changes to an arch.

11 Click in a blank area of the document to deselect the WordArt.

12 On the Standard toolbar, click the **Save** button to save the document.

Close

13 Click the **Close Window** button in the document window.

The WordArt document closes.

Lesson Wrap-Up

To finish the lesson:

Close

1 On the **File** menu, click **Exit**, or click the **Close** button in the Word window.

Word closes.

Quick Quizzes

● How do you insert Clip Art?

● How do you create Word Art?

LESSON 7

Working with Charts

After completing this lesson, you will be able to:

✓ *Add a chart to a document.*

✓ *Modify the appearance of a chart.*

When you want to compare numeric information, such as last year's quarterly sales or the time that you spent on projects last week, you can create a **chart**. Charts are graphics that use lines, bars, columns, pie slices, or other markers to represent numbers and other values. Adding a chart to a document creates visual interest and shows trends, illustrates relationships, or demonstrates how information changes over time. Microsoft Word and other Microsoft Office XP programs include Microsoft Graph Chart, a program that lets you insert and modify a chart directly in a document.

In this lesson, you'll add a chart to a memo from The Garden Company regarding its customer traffic. You'll start by creating a chart in a Word document, typing data into that chart, modifying the appearance of the chart and then importing additional data from an Excel workbook to add to the chart.

This lesson uses the practice files AddChart and ModChart that you installed from this book's CD-ROM. For details about installing the practice files, see "Using the Book's CD-ROM" at the beginning of this book.

Adding a Chart to a Document

W2002-5-2

To add a chart to a Word document, you use Microsoft Graph Chart, a program integrated with Word and other Office XP programs that lets you add, modify and format various types of charts. When you insert a chart, Microsoft Graph Chart adds a sample chart and a datasheet to the document. A **datasheet** looks similar to a table; it initially displays sample data in rows and columns. You can type to replace the sample data with your own labels and values. Because the datasheet is linked to the chart, when you change the values in the datasheet, the chart changes as well.

Your first step after inserting a datasheet and chart is to replace the sample data with your own. To do so, you work in the datasheet, entering values and labels in cells. A **cell** is where a row and column intersect.

A datasheet also contains grey buttons across the top for **column headings** and grey buttons along the left for **row headings**. When you click a heading, you select the entire column or row. To select the entire datasheet, you can click the **Select All** button, a grey box in the upper-left corner of the datasheet.

To highlight any part of a chart, you can simply click on it.

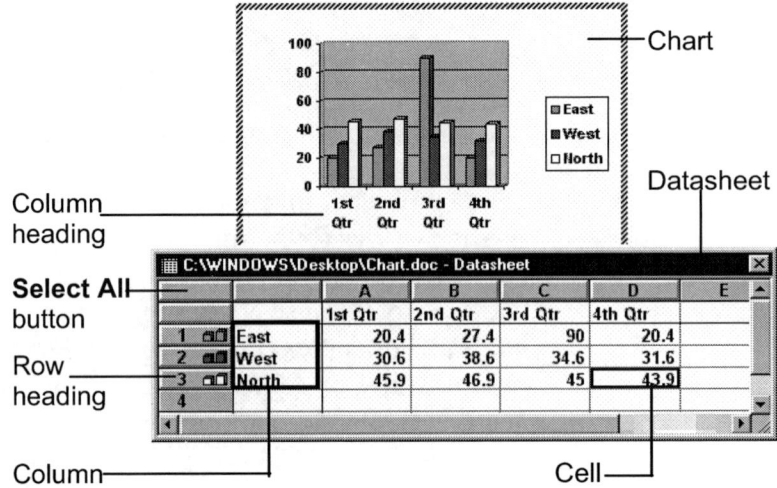

tip

If you can see your chart but not the accompanying datasheet, double-click the chart to open the datasheet.

When you insert a chart into a document, the Microsoft Graph Chart commands become available on the menu bar and toolbars so that you can work with the chart directly in your Word document.

tip

You always change data in the datasheet, but not in the chart itself. You can change the appearance of the chart, but not the values that it contains.

The owner of the Garden Company wants to add a chart to a memo that demonstrates customer traffic patterns during the first eight weeks of the year.

AddChart

Open

In this exercise, you open a document and then add a chart to the document.

1   Start Word, if necessary.

2   On the Standard toolbar, click the **Open** button.

The **Open** dialog box appears.

3   Navigate to the **SBS** folder on your hard disk, double-click the **Word** folder, double- click the **Charting** folder and then double-click the file **AddChart**.

The AddChart document opens.

4   Press ⌨Ctrl + ⌨End.

The insertion point moves to the end of the document.

To delete a chart, click on it and press [Del].

5 On the **Insert** menu, point to **Picture** and then click **Chart**.

A sample chart and datasheet appear.

6 Drag the title bar of the datasheet window so that it is positioned below the sample chart.

7 Click the **Select All** button on the datasheet (the upper-left button) and then press the [Del] key.

The sample data and sample chart are deleted.

8 Click in the first cell in row I to the left of column A, type **Morning** and then press the [Enter] key.

The heading is entered and the insertion point moves to the cell below *Morning*.

9 Type **Early Afternoon** and then press [Enter].

The insertion point moves to the cell below *Early Afternoon*.

10 Type **Evening** and then press [Enter].

The insertion point moves to the cell below *Evening*.

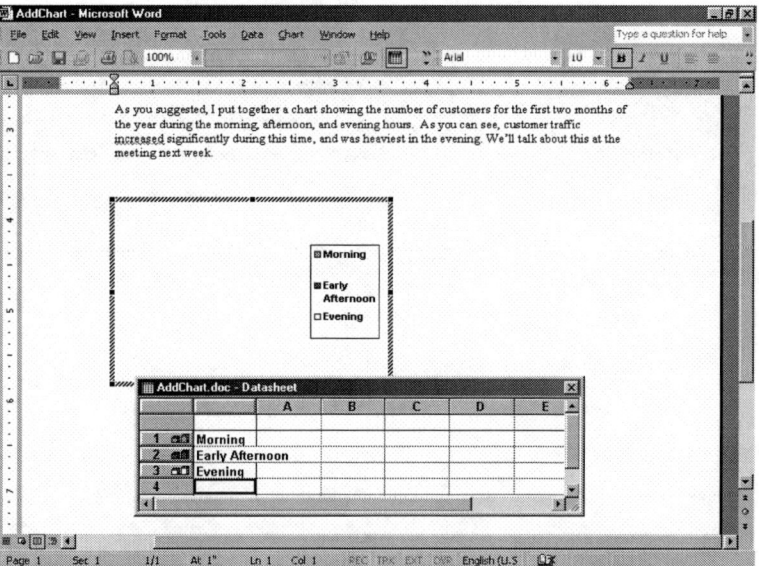

Resize pointer

◄╫►

11 In the column heading area of the datasheet, place the mouse pointer on the line to the left of the column A heading until it changes to a double-headed resize pointer and then drag the line to the right, stretching the column until the text fits in the cells.

AddChart.doc - Datasheet		A	B	C	D	
1		Morning				
2		Early Afternoon				
3		Evening				
4						

tip

You can also double-click the vertical line between column headings to resize the column to fit the longest item in the column cells.

12 Click in the cell in column A in the row above row 1. Type **Week 1** and then press the $\boxed{\text{Tab}}$ key.

Week 1 is added to the chart and the insertion point moves one cell to the right.

13 Type **Week 2** and then press $\boxed{\text{Tab}}$.

Week 2 is added to the chart and the insertion point moves one cell to the right.

14 Type **Week 3** and then press $\boxed{\text{Tab}}$.

Week 3 is added to the chart and the insertion point moves one cell to the right.

15 Type **Week 4** and then press $\boxed{\text{Enter}}$.

Week 4 is added to the chart. The data labels for the chart appear in columns A through D.

	A	B	C	D
	Week 1	Week 2	Week 3	Week 4
1 Morning				
2 Early Afternoon				
3 Evening				
4				

16 Click the first empty cell in the second row under column A and then type the following data into the chart's datasheet:

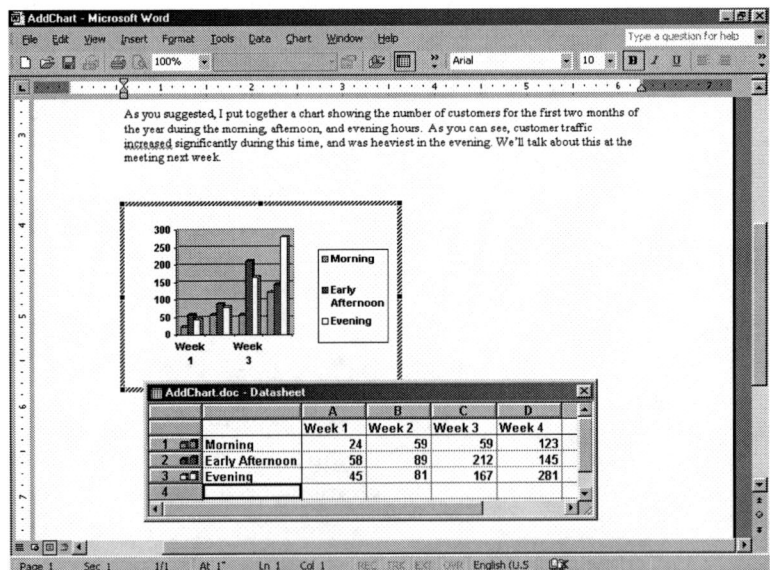

17 Click in the cell in column B, in row 3 (which contains *81*), type **79** to change the data and then press [Enter].

tip

To edit individual characters in a cell, double-click the cell to place the insertion point and then edit the text as you would in Word.

18 Click a blank area of the document to deselect the chart.

The datasheet closes and the chart is deselected.

19 On the Standard toolbar, click the **Save** button to save the document.

Close

20 Click the **Close Window** button in the document window.

The AddChart document closes.

Modifying the Appearance of a Chart

W2002-5-2

If the appearance of your chart doesn't fit your needs, you can change the chart's type, colours, borders, fonts, font sizes and chart elements. When you change the chart type, you choose one of 18 different ways to present your data. Choose the chart type that best suits the purpose of your data. For example, to show how data changes over time, you can choose a column chart. To show how parts relate to the whole, choose a pie chart. You can use the **Chart Type** list on the Standard toolbar or the **Chart Type** dialog box to choose one of the chart types. To create a customised chart, use the **Chart Type** dialog box.

In addition to changing a chart's type, you can change the appearance of the chart and its elements, such as the title, gridlines, legend and colours. You start by selecting the chart and then selecting the element that you want to modify. You can then move, resize, or format the selected element. To move a selected chart or chart item, you point to the chart or element and then drag it to another location. To resize a selected chart or chart item, you drag a sizing handle.

When you select part or all of a chart, you can use the chart buttons on Graph's Standard toolbar to format the chart, including those elements. For example, use the **Fill Colour** button to change the colour of chart elements, such as a **data marker-**the bar or area that represents a value in the datasheet-and the **plot area-**the area that includes the data markers and the category (x) and value (y) axes. Besides changing the colour of an element, you can change its pattern, called a **fill effect**. For example, you can apply a striped pattern to a **data series**, which is a group of related data markers.

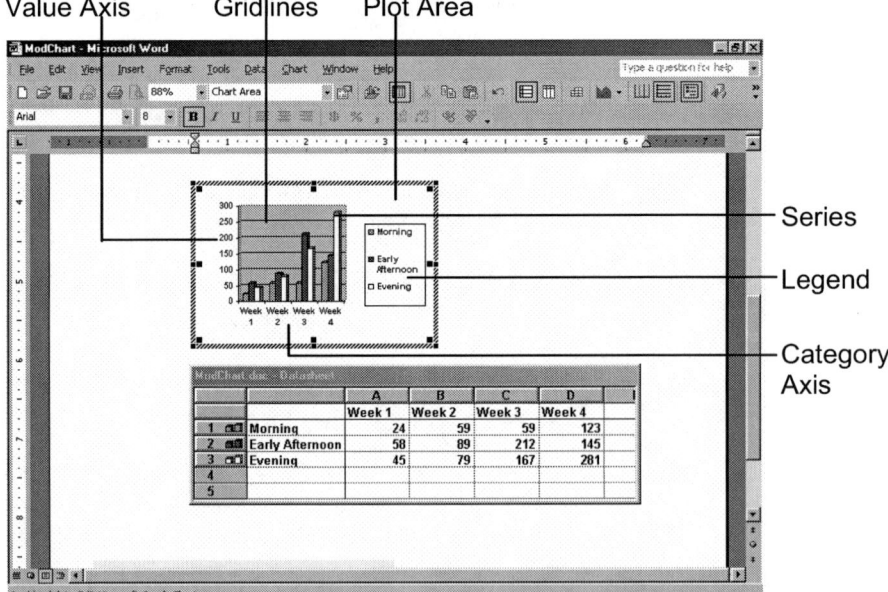

Value Axis   Gridlines   Plot Area   Series   Legend   Category Axis

Some chart elements in Microsoft Graph Chart help you interpret the chart data. For example, if your chart contains a lot of data, you can add **gridlines** to make it easier to view and evaluate the data. If the gridlines make the chart cluttered, you can remove them. A **legend** identifies the patterns or colours assigned to the data. By default, the legend appears to the right of the chart, but you can change this position. You can also clarify the data in a chart by adding labels to identify what each data series represents. If you have a small set of data, you might find it helpful to see the numeric values along with the graphical representations of the data. For line, area, column and bar charts, you can display a **data table**, a grid attached to a chart that shows the data used to create the chart.

Now that the owner of The Garden Company has added a chart to her memo, she wants to enhance its appearance and make it easier to interpret.

ModChart

In this exercise, you modify the appearance of a chart by changing its chart type and resizing it. Then you change the colour of the plot area and apply a pattern to a data series. You hide and show gridlines, move the legend and add labels to identify the data series. In addition, you add a data table to show the numeric values along with the graphic representations of the data and then you format the data table.

Open

1   On the Standard toolbar, click the **Open** button.

The **Open** dialog box appears.

2   Navigate to the **SBS** folder on your hard disk, double-click the **Word** folder, double- click the **Charting** folder and then double-click the **ModChart** file.

The ModChart document opens.

3   Scroll down the document and then double-click the chart to activate it.

The chart and datasheet appear along with Graph's toolbars and menus.

Toolbar Options

If you right-click in the **Chart Area** during editing, you can open the **Chart Type** dialog box and modify the chart type.

Chart Type
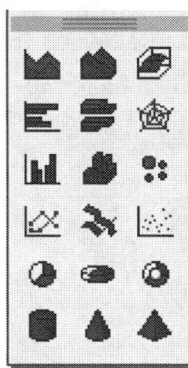

If you right-click in the Chart Area during editing you can open the **3D-View** dialog box.

4 Click **Toolbar Options** on one of the toolbars and then click **Show Buttons on Two Rows**.

The Standard and Formatting toolbars appear on two rows.

5 On the Standard toolbar, click the **Chart Type** down arrow.

The list of chart types appears, as shown in the following illustration.

Area Chart

6 Click the **Area Chart** button (the first button in the first row).

The chart type changes to an area chart, which compares data with areas of colour instead of columns.

7 On the right border of the chart, drag the middle sizing handle to the right until the chart is roughly as wide as your memo.

Now the labels for the weeks have more space between them, making the chart easier to read.

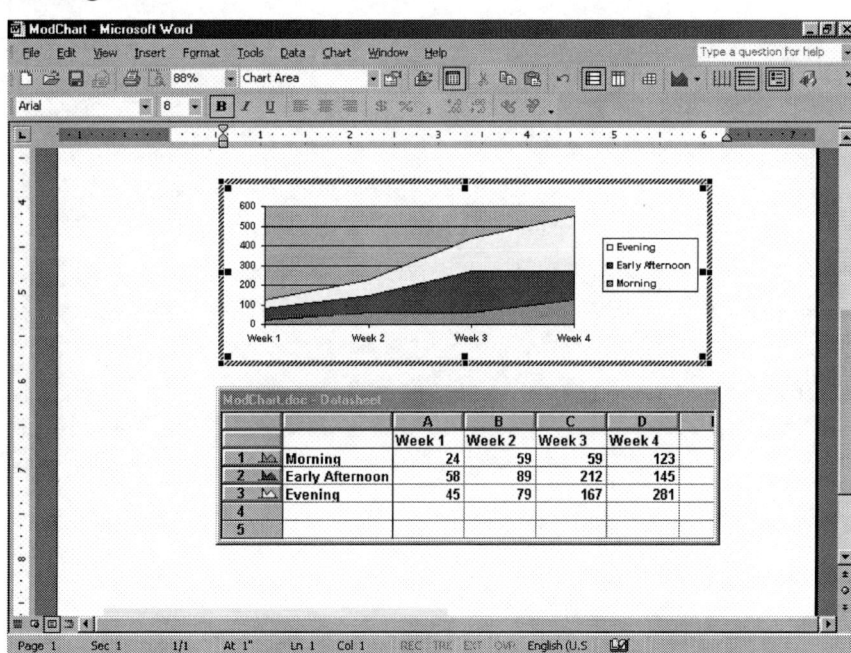

8 Point to the grey area of the chart to display the *Plot Area* ScreenTip.

9 Click the grey plot area to select the area.

Fill Colour

10 On the Standard toolbar, click the **Fill Colour** down arrow to display a colour menu.

11 Click the **Light Green** colour box (fifth row, fourth column).

The background of the chart changes to light green.

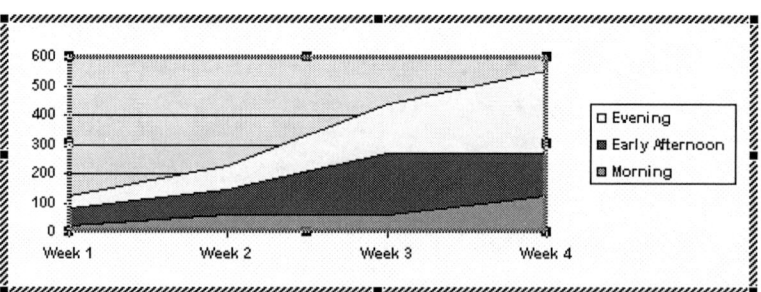

12 Point to the middle series (maroon colour) area of the chart to display the *Series "Early Afternoon"* ScreenTip and then click the Early Afternoon series in the chart to select it.

Small black squares appear around the selected area.

Format Data
Series

13 On the Standard toolbar, click the **Format Data Series** button.

The **Format Data Series** dialog box appears, showing the **Patterns** tab.

tip

You can double-click a chart element to display the **Format Data Series** dialog box.

14 Click **Fill Effects** to open the **Fill Effects** dialog box.

15 Click the **Pattern** tab to display pattern fill effects and then click the 25% pattern (first column, fourth row).

Click this
pattern

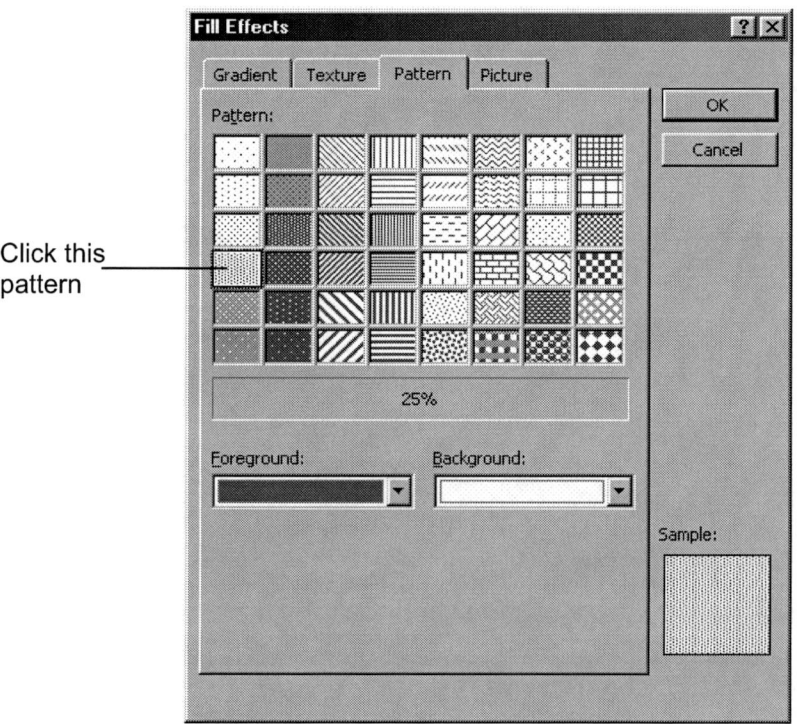

16 Click **OK** to close the **Fill Effects** dialog box and then click **OK** to close the **Format Data Series** dialog box.

The Early Afternoon series changes to a light dotted pattern.

Value Axis
Gridlines

17 On the Standard toolbar, click the **Value Axis Gridlines** button to remove the horizontal gridlines from the chart.

18 On the **Chart** menu, click **Chart Options**.

The **Chart Options** dialog box appears, showing the **Gridlines** tab.

19   In the **Value (Y) axis** area, select the **Major gridlines** check box to show horizontal gridlines.

20   Click the **Legend** tab and then click the **Top** option.

The legend is moved to the top of the chart.

21   Click the **Data Labels** tab, select the **Series name** check box and then click **OK**.

The **Chart Options** dialog box closes and a label appears next to each data series.

22   Drag the lower-middle resize handle down to increase the size of the chart.

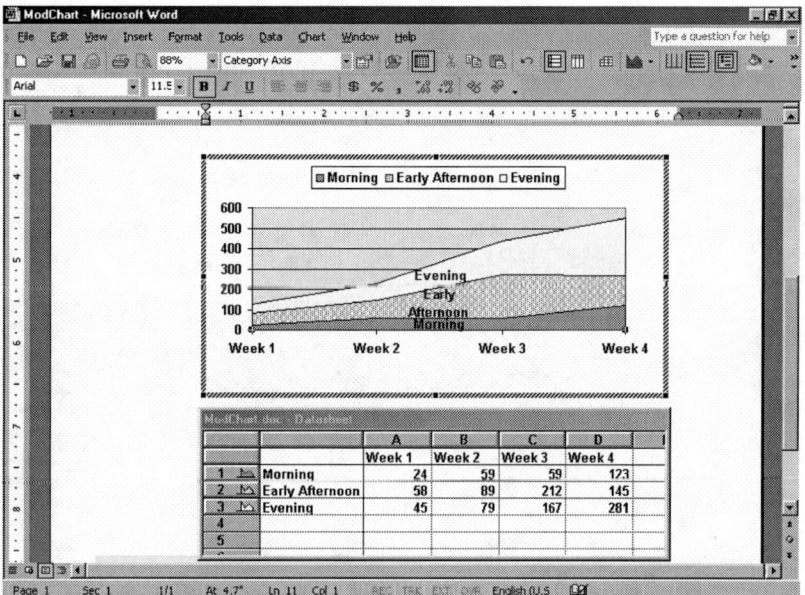

Legend

23   On the Standard toolbar, click the **Legend** button to hide the legend.

24   On the Standard toolbar, click the **Data Table** button.

Data Table

A data table is inserted below the chart.

25   Double-click the data table.

The **Format Data Table** dialog box appears, showing the **Patterns** tab.

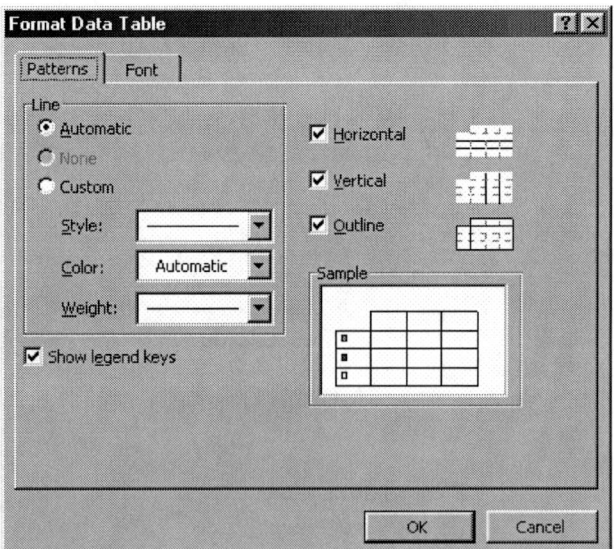

26   Click the **Colour** down arrow and then click the **Blue** colour box (second row, sixth column).

27   Click the **Font** tab, click **10 in the Size box** and then click **OK**.

The data table text is smaller, allowing it all to fit in the table.

View Datasheet

28   On the Standard toolbar, click the **View Datasheet** button to hide the datasheet and then click outside the chart to deselect it.

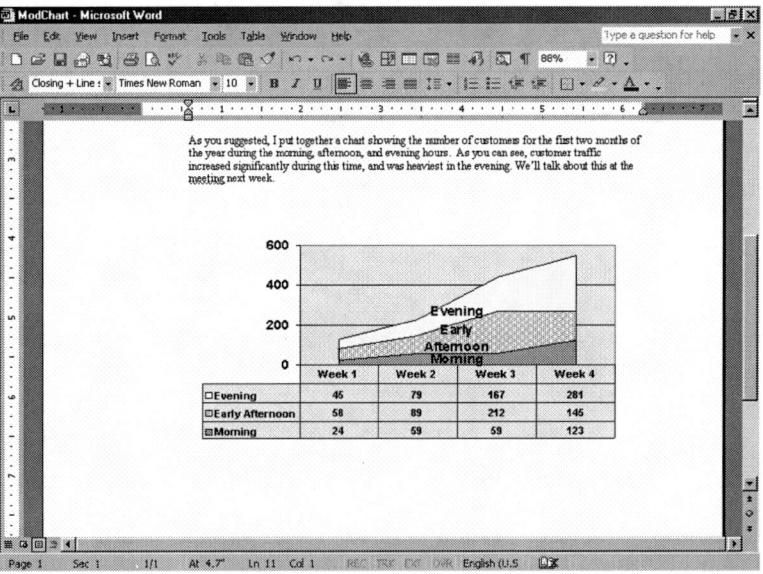

29   On the Standard toolbar, click the **Save** button to save the document.

Close

30   Click the **Close Window** button in the document window.

The ModChart document closes.

Lesson Wrap-Up

To finish the lesson:

Close

1   On the **File** menu, click **Exit**, or click the **Close** button in the Word window.

Word closes.

Quick Quizzes

- What is a chart?

- How do you insert a chart?

- How do you change the chart type?

- What is the plot area of a chart?

- How do you display the data table?

LESSON 8

Collaborating with Others

After completing this lesson, you will be able to:

✓ *Compare and merge documents.*

✓ *Review comments in a document.*

After you create a draft of a document, you might distribute it to your co-workers and ask for their comments and revisions. Collaborating with others in this way helps you produce accurate and thorough documents.

Word lets you distribute a document to reviewers electronically so that they can read, revise and comment on the document without printing it. Reviewers edit the document using the Track Changes feature so that you can see what they've changed. Reviewers can also insert **comments**, which are notes about text or other parts of the document. If you don't want reviewers to edit your work, you can protect a document so that others can only read it. For greater protection, you can assign a password so that only those who know the password can open the document. When reviewers return their comments and changes to you, you can merge all the revisions and comments into the original document and then review the changes, accepting or rejecting the changes and comments as appropriate.

You can review changes in Word by using the **Reviewing toolbar**, which contains buttons that let you accept and reject changes and comments and by using the **Reviewing Pane,** which shows information related to the changes and comments in your document.

In this lesson, an assistant at The Garden Company collaborates with the head buyer to revise a memo and related documents. The assistant tracks his changes, reviews comments and merges, accepts and rejects other changes. He also protects other documents and then he sends all the documents to the head buyer via e-mail.

This lesson uses the practice files CompareMerge, Merge1, Merge2 and RevComment that you installed from this book's CD-ROM. For details about installing the practice files, see "Using the Book's CD-ROM" at the beginning of this book.

Comparing and Merging Documents

W2002-6-1
W2002e-6-2

You can modify the formatting of changes by clicking **Options** on the **Tools** menu and then the **Track Changes** tab.

CompareMerge Merge1 Merge2

Compare and merge documents
new for
OfficeXP

If you want to compare an earlier version of a document with the current version of a document, you can compare the documents and then merge the changes into one document. For example, if you ask an associate to edit a document, but he doesn't track changes while editing, you can compare his edited document to your original to see what changes he made.

When you compare and merge documents, Word shows the differences between them as tracked changes. If multiple reviewers return their changes and comments in separate documents, you can merge all their changes into a single document and review their changes from that single document. You then can review changes from a specific reviewer.

An assistant at The Garden Company is ready to revise the memo for the head buyer. The memo lists price changes for non-plant products within The Garden Company.

In this exercise, you merge the document with two other versions of the document.

1   On the Standard toolbar, click the **Open** button.

The **Open** dialog box appears.

2   Navigate to the **SBS** folder on your hard disk, double-click the **Word** folder, double- click the **Collaborating** folder and then double-click the **CompareMerge** file.

The CompareMerge document opens.

3   On the **Tools** menu, click **Compare and Merge Documents**.

The **Compare and Merge Documents** dialog box appears.

4   Navigate to the **Collaborating** folder.

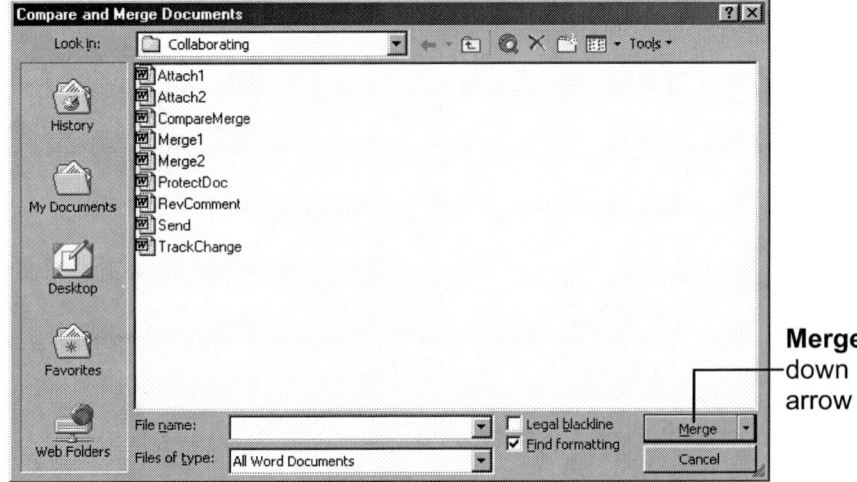

Merge down arrow

5   Click **Merge1**, click the **Merge** down arrow and then click **Merge into current document**.

The deletions and changes from the document appear on the screen in the current document. The colour of each revision indicates a different reviewer.

tip

When you compare versions of a document, you see reviewers' changes even if the reviewers did not track their changes as they edited.

6 On the **Tools** menu, click **Compare and Merge Documents**, navigate to the **Collaborating** folder, click **Merge2**, click the **Merge** down arrow and then click **Merge into current document**.

The deletions and changes from the documents appear on the screen in the current document with the other changes.

7 Scroll down the document to see the product information.

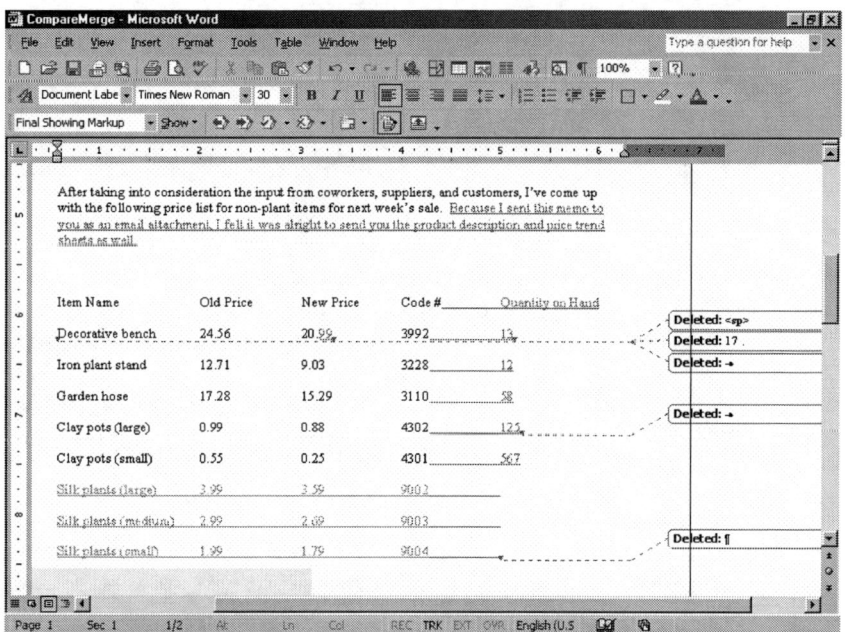

The colours of the tracked changes above might not be the same as the ones that you see on your screen.

8 On the Reviewing toolbar, click the **Show** down arrow, point to Reviewers and then click **Jill B**.

The revisions made by the Jill B. reviewer are hidden.

9 On the Reviewing toolbar, click the **Show** down arrow, point to Reviewers and then click **All Reviewers**.

The revisions made by all reviewers appear.

10 Type 132, 139 and 167 as the Quantity On Hand for the large, medium and small silk plants.

11 Scroll up to the top of the document, if necessary.

The title of the document has been changed by one of the reviewers.

12 On the Reviewing toolbar, click the **Show** down arrow and then click **Formatting**.

Only insertions and deletions, not formatting changes, appear in the document.

13 Triple-click the *Memorandum* paragraph to select the entire paragraph and then press the ⬚ Del ⬚ key.

The second title from the document is deleted, leaving the one merged from the Merge1 document.

Next

14 On the Reviewing toolbar, click the **Next** button.

The added text *for Next Sales Period* is selected.

Accept Change

15 On the Reviewing toolbar, click the **Accept Change** button to accept the change and then click the **Next** button to find the next revision.

The added sentence in the first paragraph is selected.

Reject Change/Delete Comment

16 On the Reviewing toolbar, click the **Reject Change/Delete Comment** button to reject the change.

The added sentence change is removed.

17 On the Reviewing toolbar, click the **Display for Review** down arrow, click **Final** and then scroll through the document.

The document appears with all the current changes and without the revision marks.

18 On the Reviewing toolbar, click the **Display for Review** down arrow and then click **Final Showing Markup**.

The document appears with all the revision marks.

19 On the Reviewing toolbar, click the **Accept Change** down arrow and then click **Accept All Changes in Document**.

The changes are accepted.

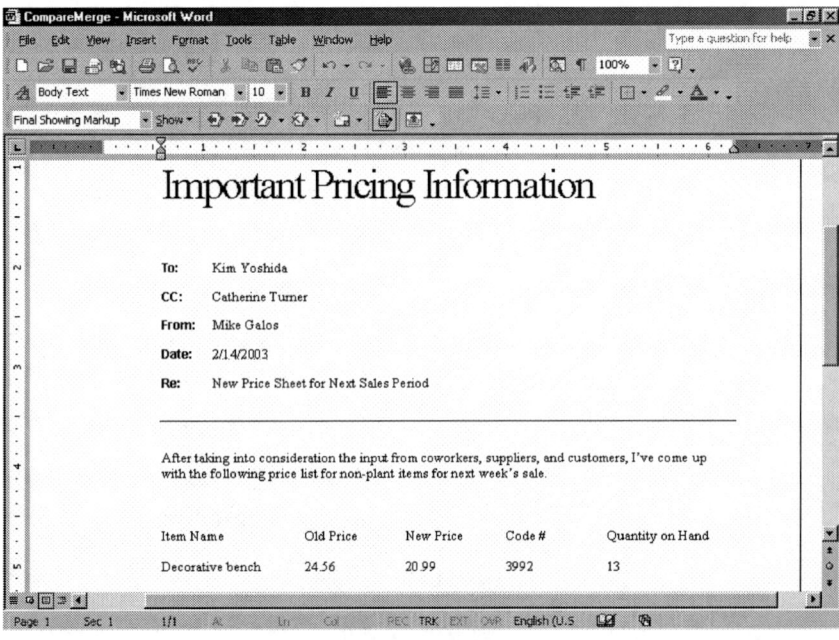

20 On the Standard toolbar, click the **Save** button to save the document.

Close

21 Click the **Close Window** button in the document window.

The CompareMerge document closes.

Reviewing Comments in a Document

W2002-6-2

In addition to tracking changes, you can insert **comments**, which are notes or annotations that you or a reviewer adds to a document without changing the document text. To insert a comment, you select the text that you want to comment on and then click the **New Comment** button on the Reviewing toolbar. Type your comment in the comment balloon or the Reviewing Pane. Word inserts coloured brackets around commented text and displays comments in a balloon in the margin of the document or in the Reviewing Pane.

Reviewing toolbar
new for
OfficeXP

To view comments, read the text in the comment balloons. You can also point to commented text to see a ScreenTip showing both the name of the person who made the comment and the date and time of the comment. To edit or delete a comment, right-click the commented text and then click **Edit Comment** or **Delete Comment**. To review comments, click the **Next Comment** and **Previous Comment** buttons to move from one comment to another. To respond to a comment, click in the comment balloon or the comment text in the document and then click the **New Comment** button. Type your response in the new comment balloon that appears.

If Word cannot display the complete text of a comment in a balloon, you can open the Reviewing Pane to see the entire comment. If you find the comment balloons distracting, you can turn them off and work with comments only in the Reviewing Pane. To show or hide balloons, on the **Tools** menu, click **Options** to open the **Options** dialog box, click the **Track Changes** tab and then select or clear the **Use balloons** check box. To show or hide the Reviewing Pane, click the **Reviewing Pane** button on the Reviewing toolbar. In addition to providing information about comments in the document, the Reviewing Pane tracks changes to the main part of the document, to headers and footers and their text boxes, to text boxes themselves and to footnotes and endnotes.

To display comments in **Normal** or **Outline** view, activate the **Reviewing Pane**

RevComment

In this exercise, you show and review comments in a document, add a comment, delete one that is no longer needed and then hide the remaining comment.

1 On the Standard toolbar, click the **Open** button.

The **Open** dialog box appears.

Open

2 Navigate to the **SBS** folder on your hard disk, double-click the **Word** folder, double- click the **Collaborating** folder and then double-click the **RevComment** file.

The RevComment document opens.

Web Layout View

3 Click the **Web Layout View** button to switch to Web Layout view.

4 On the **View** menu, click **Markup** to show comments and changes and to display the Reviewing toolbar.

Next

5 On the Reviewing toolbar, click the **Next** button to display the first comment in the document and then scroll down to display the entire comment.

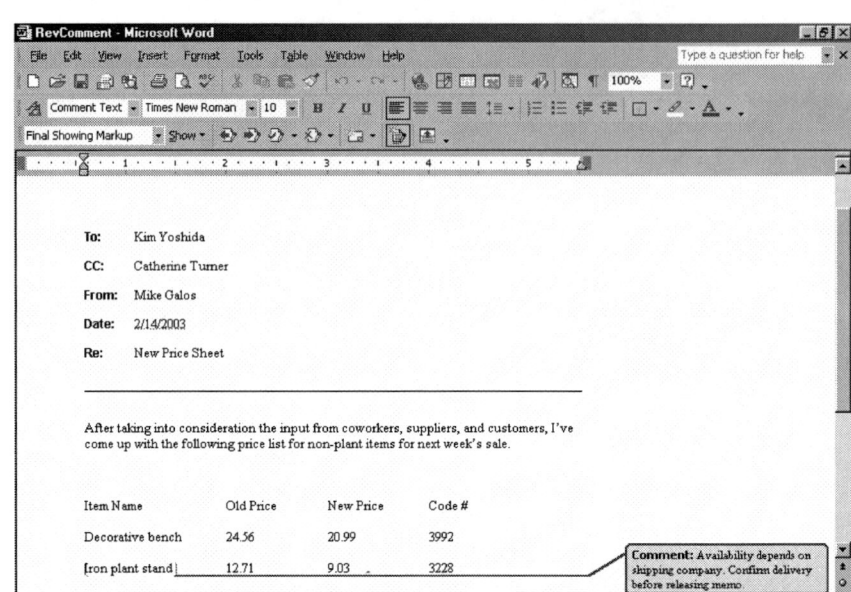

The insertion point appears in the first balloon comment and brackets appear around the text *Iron plant stand*. The brackets show where comments have been inserted.

6 On the Reviewing toolbar, click the **Next** button to display the next comment in the document.

The insertion point appears in the next balloon comment and brackets appear around the text *Clay pots (small)*.

7 Point to the text *Iron plant stand* and then read the ScreenTip.

The ScreenTip displays information about who inserted the comment and when.

8 Drag the horizontal scroll bar to the right, if necessary, to read the comments along the right side of the document.

9 Drag to select the *Garden hose* text.

New Comment

10 On the Reviewing toolbar, click the **New Comment** button.

Word adds brackets around the *Garden hose* text and inserts a comment balloon in the right margin.

11 In the comment balloon, type **Preferred customers receive an extra 10% discount on hoses.**

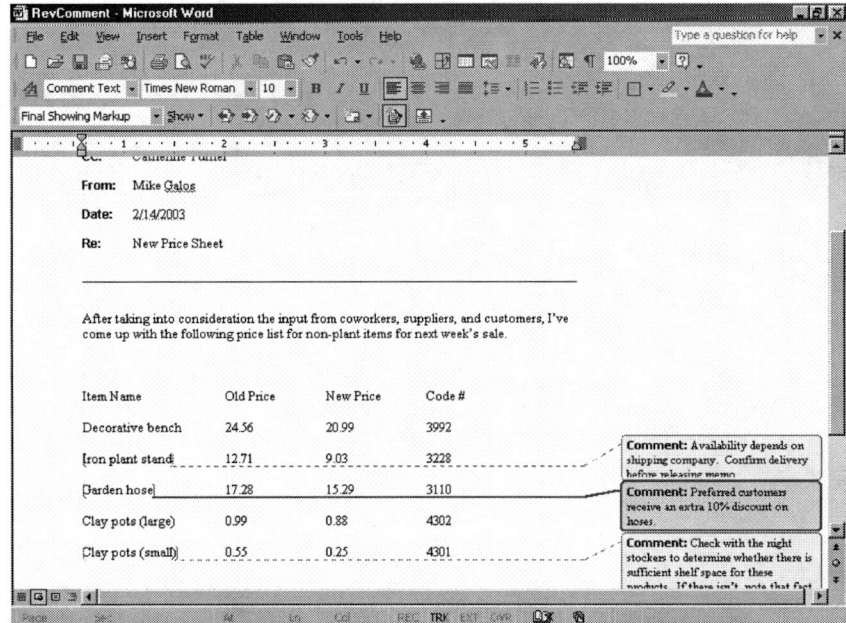

12 Click a blank area of the document to deselect the comment.

13 Right-click anywhere on the *Iron plant stand* text and then click **Delete Comment** to delete the comment from the screen.

Reviewing Pane

14 On the Reviewing toolbar, click the **Reviewing Pane** button.

The Reviewing Pane opens at the bottom of the Word window, showing the remaining comments about the garden hoses and clay pots.

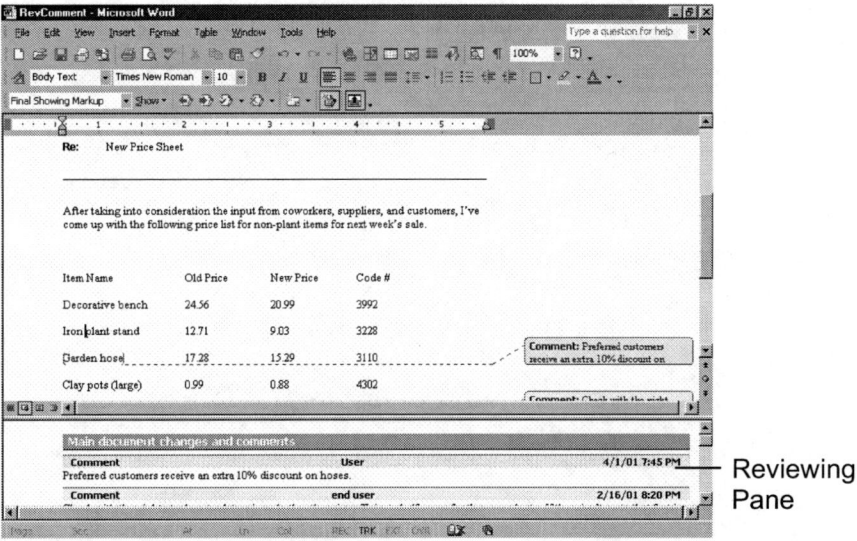

Resize pointer

tip

To change the size of the Reviewing Pane, point to the top edge of the Reviewing Pane until the pointer changes to a resize pointer and then drag the edge.

15 Click to the right of the last word (*intact*) in the second comment, press 〔 Space 〕, type your initials, type a colon (:), press 〔 Space 〕 and then type **I'm not sure if there is enough shelf space.**

The text appears in the Reviewing Pane for the selected comment.

16   On the Reviewing toolbar, click the **Reviewing Pane** button to close the Reviewing Pane.

17   Right-click the *Clay pots (small)* text and then click **Edit Comment**.

The insertion point appears at the end of the comment attached to the *Clay pots (small)* text.

New Comment

18   On the Reviewing toolbar, click the **New Comment** button to create a new balloon comment in response to the other comment.

Dotted lines connect both comments.

19   Type I checked with the shipping company. They are ready to go.

The text appears in the balloon comment.

20   Double-click 3992 in the decorative bench code to select the number.

21   On the Reviewing toolbar, click the **New Comment** button to create a new balloon comment.

22   Type Kim, Is this product code correct?.

The text appears in the balloon comment.

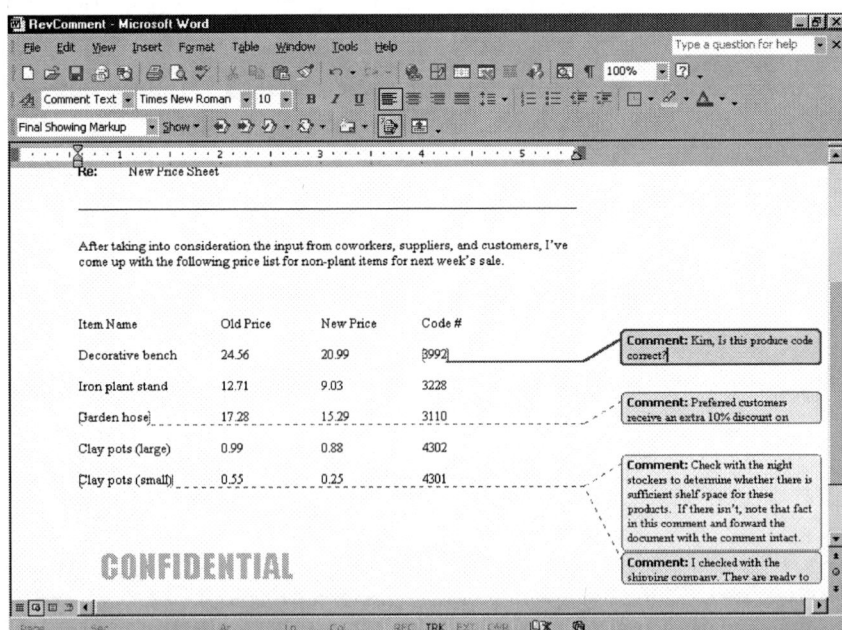

tip

If you have a sound card and a microphone installed on your computer, you can record voice comments, which are attached as sound objects to the text in the document. To insert a voice comment, on the Reviewing toolbar, click the **New Comment** down arrow, click **Voice Comment** and then record the voice comment. If an alert appears asking whether you want to update the sound object, click **Yes**.

23   On the Reviewing toolbar, click the **Show** down arrow and then click **Comments** to hide them.

Close

24   On the Standard toolbar, click the **Save** button to save the document.

25   Click the **Close Window** button in the document window.

The RevComment document closes.

Lesson Wrap-Up

To finish the lesson:

Close

1   On the **File** menu, click **Exit**, or click the **Close** button in the Word window.

Word closes.

Quick Quizzes

● How do you compare and merge documents?

● How do you insert and review comments?

● What does "Mail Recipient (for Review)" mean?

LESSON 9

Working with Documents on the Web

After completing this lesson, you will be able to:

✓ *Create a Web document containing links.*

If you have ever explored the Web to find sports scores or to research a topic, you know that the Web is an appealing, informative and immediate medium. Your documents can find a broader audience if you transform them into Web pages and let others read them on the Web. For example, if you develop materials such as newsletters, brochures and flyers, you can publish them on the Web and your readers can view them in a browser such as Microsoft Internet Explorer.

Although professional Web page designers use special programs, such as Microsoft FrontPage, to design sophisticated Web pages, Word is a good choice for creating simple Web pages or for converting existing documents to Web pages. Word lets you save a document as a Web page, preview it in your Web browser and then modify it as necessary. You can also add **hyperlinks** to the document, which you and others can click to link to other documents, Web pages, or e- mail addresses. To help others explore your Web pages, you can create a **link bar**, which includes **Back** and **Next** buttons to guide users through a series of pages. You can also apply a **digital signature** to confirm that your Web document has not been changed since you created it.

In this lesson, you'll create a Web document from a Word document and then add links to it. You'll also open an existing Web document and modify it. Then you'll add a digital signature to a document.

This lesson uses the practice files CreateWeb and OtherLogos that you installed from this book's CD-ROM. For details about installing the practice files, see "Using the Book's CD-ROM" at the beginning of this book.

Creating a Web Document Containing Links

W2002-6-3
W2002e-6-3
W2002e-6-4

You can save any Word document as a **Web page**, which is a special document designed to be viewed in a program called a Web browser. Most of the formatting in your Word document will be preserved when you view the document as a Web page in your browser. However, some formatting is not converted, such as text wrapping around pictures and objects and other features are not supported by all Web browsers: for example, table formatting, character formatting, page layout features and security and document protection.

If you know which Web browser your viewers will be using, it's a good idea to optimize your Web page for that browser. Word lets you specify the browser that viewers of your Web documents are using and then it disables any features that won't appear in that Web browser. To see how your document will appear in a Web browser, you can preview it as a Web page and then edit as necessary. When you're satisfied with the results, you save the document as a Web page. You can also click the **Web Layout View** button above the status bar to see how a document appears as a Web page.

You can convert existing Word documents to Web pages using the **Save as Web Page** command on the **File** menu. To create a new Web page, you can use the **Web Page Wizard** or a Web page template. For a multipage **Web site** (a collection of related Web pages), complete with navigation tools and a professionally designed theme, you can use the **Web Page Wizard**, which guides you through the steps of creating Web pages. To create a particular kind of Web page, such as one for frequently asked questions or personal information, you can use a Web template. To use the **Web Page Wizard** or a Web page template, on the **File** menu, click **New**, click **General Templates** in the **New Document** task pane, click the **Web Pages** tab, double-click **Web Page Wizard** and then follow the instructions in the wizard, or double-click a Web template.

Filtered Web page and Web archive **new for OfficeXP**

You can save a Word document as a Web page, a filtered Web page, or a Web archive. A Web page is a document in HTML (Hypertext Markup Language, the markup language of tags which determine how text and graphics are displayed in a browser), while a **filtered Web page** is a document in HTML optimized without Microsoft Office-specific HTML tags. A **Web archive** saves all the elements of a Web site, including text and graphics, into a single document with the .mht extension. When you save a Word document as a Web page, Word changes any unsupported formatting, such as table borders, background and animated text, so that Web browsers can display the information. To make your Web page viewable by others over the Internet, you need to save it on a **Web server**, a process known as **publishing**. To publish a Web document to a Web server, your computer needs to have access to a Web server using an Internet or network connection. Once you have a connection, you can use the **Web Folders** icon in the **Save As** dialog box to navigate to a Web server and then save the Web document in the same way that you save a document to your hard disk.

Web pages use hyperlinks--text, graphics, or other objects--that you can click to perform an action, such as opening another Web page or document. You can insert hyperlinks (also called **links**) into a Web document or any other type of Word document to link to another Web page, file, e-mail address, or **bookmark**, which is a location in a document that you identify and name for future reference. To insert a hyperlink, you click the **Insert Hyperlink** button on the Standard toolbar to display the **Insert Hyperlink** dialog box. Use the buttons in the **Link to bar** to set up a link to another file or Web page, to another place in the document, such as a heading or bookmark, to a new document, or to an e-mail address. To link to another Web page, you specify a **Uniform Resource Locator** (URL), which is a unique address for the Web page, such as *www.microsoft.com*. A URL consists of three parts: the prefix *http://*, which indicates a Web address; a network identification, such as *www* for World Wide Web; and a Web site name, or domain name, such as *microsoft.com*.

Hyperlinks appear in Word documents as blue underlined text, which is similar to the way that they appear in browsers. To edit a hyperlink, you right-click it and then choose a command from the shortcut menu to change the destination of the hyperlink, to change the display text, or to convert the hypcrlink to regular text.

When you insert a hyperlink into a document, you can use the **Set Target Frame** dialog box to control how the linked page is displayed in the document. You can display the linked page in the same window as the original page, in a new window, or in a **frame**, which is a window region on a Web page. You can follow a hyperlink in any Word document by holding down the [Ctrl] key and then clicking the link. When you view the Web document in your browser, you can simply click the link to follow it.

The head buyer for the Garden Company created a document containing sales ads and wants to convert the document into a Web document. To make it easy to access logos that are mentioned in the sales ads document, the buyer will insert hyperlinks into a document that contains company logos.

CreateWeb,
OtherLogos

In this exercise, you set options for displaying a document in Microsoft Internet Explorer 5.0 or later, preview and save the document as a Web page and insert, test and modify a hyperlink.

To complete this exercise, you need a Web browser; Internet Explorer 5.0 or later is recommended. You can use another browser, but the functionality and settings might be different.

1   Start Word, if necessary.

Open

2   On the Standard toolbar, click the **Open** button.

The **Open** dialog box appears.

3   Navigate to the **SBS** folder on your hard disk, double-click the **Word** folder, double- click the **WorkingWeb** folder and then double-click the **CreateWeb** file.

The CreateWeb document opens in Print Layout view.

4   On the **Tools** menu, click **Options**.

The **Options** dialog box appears.

5   Click the **General** tab, if necessary and then click **Web Options**.

The **Web Options** dialog box appears.

To change the screen dimensions of Web pages, click the **Pictures** tab on the **Web Options** dialog box.

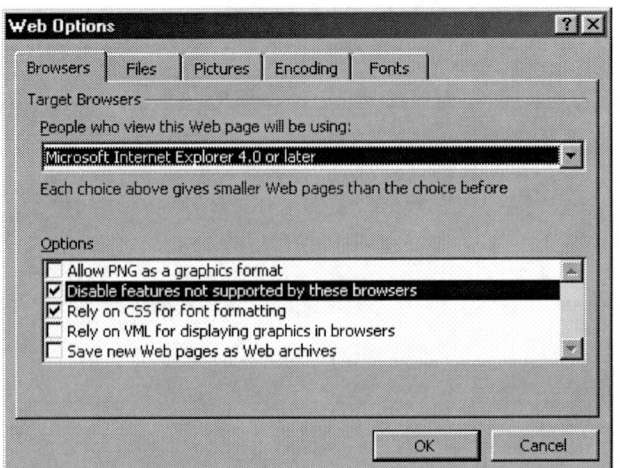

6   Click the **Browsers** tab if necessary, click the **People who view this Web page will be using** down arrow and then click **Microsoft Internet Explorer 5.0 or later**.

To display the web view of a document, from the **View** menu, click **Web Layout**.

7   In the **Options** list, verify that the **Disable features not supported by these browsers** check box is selected and then click **OK** to close the **Web Options** dialog box.

8   Click **OK** to close the **Options** dialog box.

9   On the **File** menu, click **Web Page Preview**.

The CreateWeb document opens in your Web browser.

Maximize

10   Click the **Maximize** button to maximize the Internet Explorer window.

11   On the **File** menu, click **Close** to close the Internet Explorer window.

The Word window appears.

12   On the **File** menu, click **Save as Web Page**.

The **Save As** dialog box appears.

tip

When you save a document as a Web page, you can specify a page title for the document. This title appears in the title bar of the Web browser and it can be different from the file name. To specify a Web page title, click **Change Title** in the **Save As** dialog box and then type the title in the **Page title** box.

13   Navigate to the **WorkingWeb** folder and then type **WebDoc** in the **File name** box.

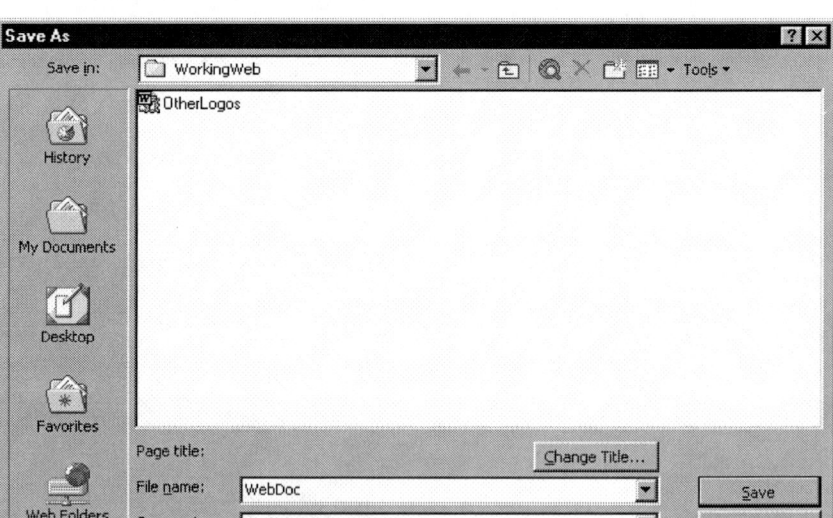

14 Click the **Save as type** down arrow and then click **Web page**.

15 Click **Save**.

A message box appears, indicating that some features in this document are not supported by Internet Explorer 5.0.

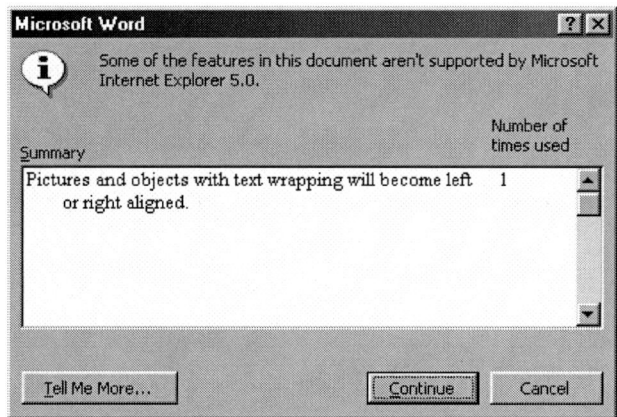

16 Click **Continue**.

The document appears in Word, this time in **Web Layout** view. The Word document is now a Web document.

17   Scroll down to see The Garden Company logo if necessary, right-click the logo and then click **Hyperlink**.

The **Insert Hyperlink** dialog box appears, displaying the WorkingWeb folder.

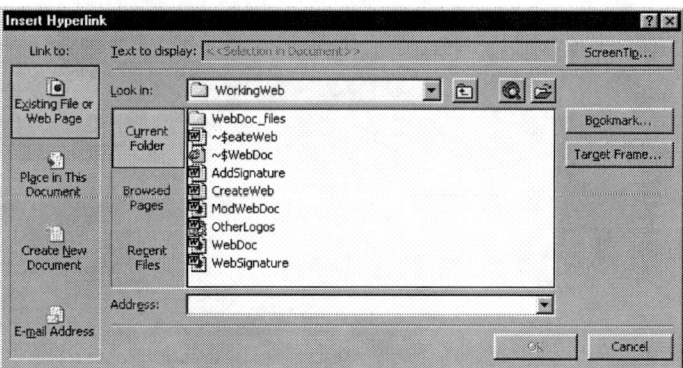

18   In the list of folders and file names, click the **OtherLogos** file and then click **Target Frame**.

The **Set Target Frame** dialog box appears with Page Default (none) as the current frame setting.

When you view your Web document in a browser and click the company logo, the OtherLogos document will open in the same window.

19   Click **OK** to accept the default selection, click **OK** to close the **Insert Hyperlink** dialog box and then point to the logo again.

Word displays a ScreenTip that shows the path of this hyperlink to the OtherLogos file.

It's not necessary to hold down Ctrl in Internet Explorer.

20 Hold down Ctrl and then click the logo.

The OtherLogos file is displayed in your browser window.

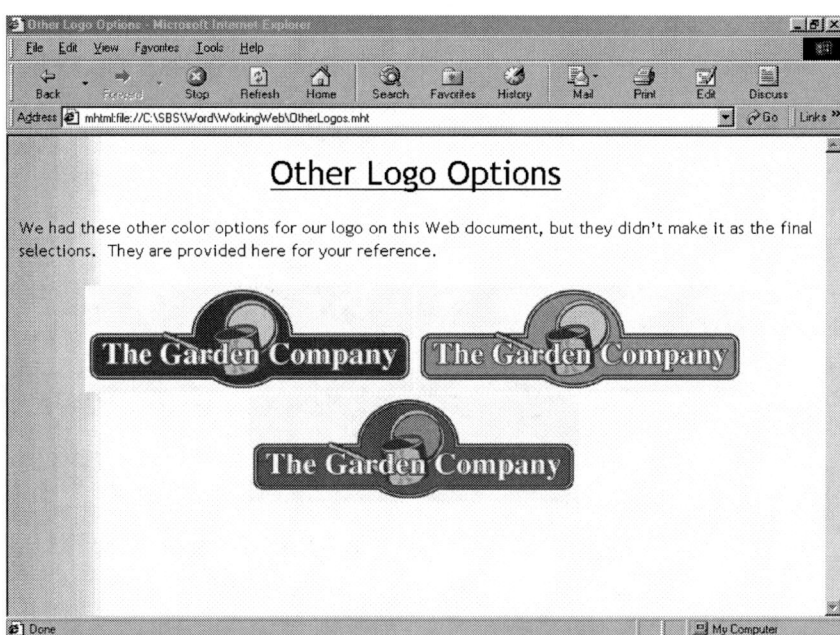

21 On the **File** menu, click **Close** to close the Internet Explorer window.

The Word window appears. In the first line of the document, the phrase The Garden Company's is underlined to indicate that it is a hyperlink.

22 Click to the left of The Garden Company's hyperlink to select the text box containing it, point to the hyperlink and then read the ScreenTip.

The ScreenTip shows the target Web address as http://www.msn.com.

23 Right-click the hyperlink and then click **Edit Hyperlink**.

The **Edit Hyperlink** dialog box appears with the current Web address for this link in the **Address** box.

24   In the **Address** box, click before the letters *msn* and then type gardenco.

You changed the link to connect to The Garden Company's Web address-*www.gardenco.msn.com*.

tip

When you type a URL as a hyperlink, you do not have to include the *http://* protocol. If you omit the protocol, your browser will add *http://* for you automatically. You only need to add the protocol—the letters before the colon—if it is something other than *http*, such as *ftp*.

25   Click **OK** to close the **Edit Hyperlink** dialog box and then point to the hyperlink again.

The ScreenTip shows that the Web address is *http://www.gardenco.msn.com*.

26   On the Standard toolbar, click the **Save** button to save the document.

Close

X

27   Click the **Close Window** button in the document window.

The WebDoc document closes.

Adding a Link Bar

Link bar
new for
OfficeXP

Once you convert a Word document to a Web or Web archive document and save it to a Web server that is running Microsoft FrontPage 2002 Server Extensions or Microsoft SharePoint, you can insert a link bar into the document. A **link bar** is a collection of graphic or text buttons representing hyperlinks to pages in your Web site and external Web sites. A link bar gives you and others who use your document a way to easily navigate around the content and features of your Web document. For example, link bars include Next and Back links, which you can click to move from one page to another in sequence. You also can add custom links in a link bar, such as one to your home page and arrange them in any order you like.

You can format and style the link bar to match the design of your Web site. For example, you can change the font of the text, add images and apply themes. You can also choose a bar type, such as rounded or rectangular, a bar style, such as 2-D or 3-D and an orientation to specify whether the link bar resides across the top or along the left side of your Web page.

You can create a link bar from scratch or create one based on an existing link bar.

important

You need access to a server running Microsoft FrontPage Version 2002 Server Extensions or Microsoft SharePoint to create link bars.

To add a link bar to a Web page:

1   On the **File** menu, click **Save as Web Page**.

    The **Save As** dialog box appears.

2   In the **Places Bar**, click **Web Folders** and then navigate to a Web server that is running Microsoft FrontPage 2002 Server Extensions or Microsoft SharePoint.

    See your network administrator or the Microsoft SharePoint documentation for instructions to access a Web server.

3   In the File name box, type a name and then click **Save**.

    Word saves the document to a Web server.

4   On the **Insert** menu, click **Web Component**.

    The **Insert Web Component** Wizard appears.

5   In the **Component type** list, click **Link Bars**.

6   In the **Choose a bar type** list, click a link bar type and then click **Next** to display the next page.

7   In the **Choose a bar style** list, click a bar style.

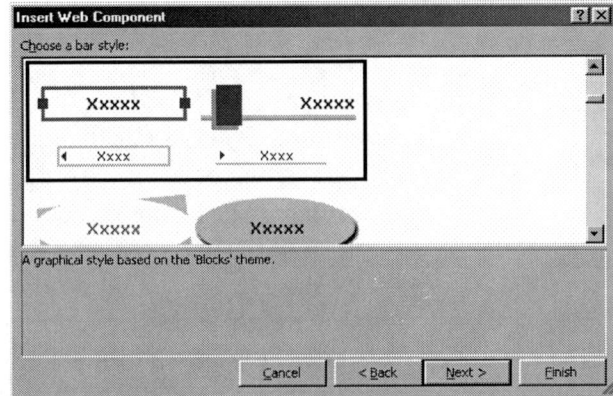

8   Click **Next** to display the next page.

9   In the **Choose an orientation** list, click an orientation (the location of the link bar on the Web page) and then click **Finish**.

    The **Link Bar Properties** dialog box appears.

10   In the **Choose existing** list, click **Create New**, type a name for your link bar in the **Name** box and then click **OK** to create a new link bar or click the name of a link bar to reuse an existing link bar.

11   Click **Add link**.

12   Select the link that you want and then type the text for the link in the **Text to display** box.

13   Click **OK** and then click **Add link** to add any more links that you want.

14   Click **Move up** or **Move down** to change the order of your links.

15   Click **OK** to add the link bar to your document.

Lesson Wrap-Up

To finish the lesson:

Close

1   On the **File** menu, click **Exit**, or click the **Close** button in the Word window.

Word closes.

Quick Quizzes

● What is a hypertext document?

● What is the purpose of a hyperlink?

● How do you insert a hyperlink?

● What is a Link bar?

● How do you change a hyperlink?

Quick Reference

Lesson 1:   Creating a Document

To start Microsoft Word

Start

1   On the taskbar, click the **Start** button.

2   On the **Start** menu, point to **Programs** and then click **Microsoft Word**.

To use the Ask A Question box

1   On the right side of the menu bar, click in the **Ask A Question** box.

2   Type a question, press 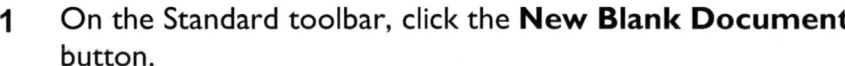 Enter and then click a topic.

New Blank Document

To create a new blank document

1   On the Standard toolbar, click the **New Blank Document** button.

To enter text

1   Click in the document to place the insertion point where you want the text to begin.

2   Type the text.

To save a new document

Save

1   On the Standard toolbar, click the **Save** button.

2   Click the **Save in** down arrow and then select a location for the file.

3   In the **File name** box, type the file name.

4   Click **Save**.

To save a file for use in another program

1   On the **File** menu, click **Save As**.

2   In the **File name** box, type a new name for the document.

3   Click the **Save as type** down arrow, click the file format that you want to use and then click **Save**.

To edit text

1   Select the text or place the insertion point where you want to edit.

2   Press Del or Backspace to delete text and then retype the text.

To close a document

Close

1 On the **File** menu, click **Close**, or click the **Close Window** button in the document window

To find and replace text

1 On the **Edit** menu, click **Replace** to open the **Find and Replace** dialog box.

2 In the **Find what** box, type the text you want to find.

3 Press ⌈Tab⌋ to move the insertion point to the **Replace with** box, type the text you want to use instead, if desired and then click **Find Next**.

4 Click **Replace** or **Replace All** to replace text or **Find Next** to find text.

5 Click **OK** and then click the **Close** button.

Lesson 2: Changing the Look of Text in a Document

To change the appearance of text

1 Select the text you want to change.

2 On the Formatting toolbar, click a formatting button, or on the **Format** menu, click **Reveal Formatting** to open the **Reveal Formatting** task pane and then use the links to open dialog boxes and make changes.

To insert an AutoText entry

1 On the **Insert** menu, point to **AutoText**, point to a category and then click an entry.

To format a paragraph

1 Click in the paragraph or select any part of it.

2 Apply the formats that you want from the toolbars, or on the **Format** menu, click **Paragraph** to open the **Paragraph** dialog box and then make changes.

To create a bulleted or numbered list

1 Select the text.

2 On the Formatting toolbar, click the **Numbering** button or the **Bullets** button, or on the **Format** menu, click **Bullets and Numbering** to display the **Bullets and Numbering** dialog box, click a tab and then click a bullet or numbering style.

Lesson 3: Changing the Look of a Document

To change line and page break options

1   On the **Format** menu, click **Paragraph** to display the **Paragraph** dialog box and then click the **Line and Page Breaks** tab, if necessary.

2   Select the **Widow/Orphan control** check box, if desired, select the **Keep lines together** check box, if desired and then click **OK**.

3   On the **Insert** menu, click **Break** to open the **Break** dialog box.

4   Select the option(s) you want and then click **OK**.

To add a header or footer to a document

1   On the **View** menu, click **Header and Footer**.

2   Using the Header and Footer toolbar to move around and make selections, type header and/or footer text.

3   Use the Header and Footer toolbar to format and change the header and/or footer text.

4   On the Header and Footer toolbar, click the **Close** button.

To open and use the Styles and Formatting task pane to change styles

1   Select the text you want to style.

2   On the **Format** menu, click **Styles and Formatting** to open the **Styles and Formatting** task pane.

3   In the **Styles and Formatting** task pane, point to the preview box in the **Formatting of selected text** section to display information about the current style.

4   In the **Styles and Formatting** task pane, click an option from the **Pick formatting to apply** section, or click **New Style** and then define a new style with the options in the **New Style** dialog box.

Lesson 4: Proof Reading and Printing a Document

To check the spelling and grammar in a document

Spelling and Grammar

ABC

1   On the Standard toolbar, click the **Spelling and Grammar** button.

2   Use the **Spelling and Grammar** dialog box to respond to text that is flagged.

3   Click **OK** to close the alert message that Word has finished checking the spelling and grammar in the document.

Preview

To preview a document

1   On the Standard toolbar, click the **Print Preview** button.

To print a document

1   On the **File** menu, click **Print**.

2   In the **Print** dialog box, select a printer and then choose the print options you want to use.

3   Click **OK**.

To print an envelope or label to accompany a letter document

1   Select the inside address at the top of the document.

2   On the **Tools** menu, point to **Letters and Mailings** and then click **Envelopes and Labels**.

3   In the **Envelopes and Labels** dialog box, click the **Envelopes** tab or **Labels** tab, select the options you want to use and then click **Print**.

Lesson 5:   Presenting Information in Tables and Columns

To create a new table

1   Click in the document to place the insertion point where you want to create a table.

2   On the **Table** menu, point to **Insert** and then click **Table**.

3   Type the number of columns and rows you want to use and then click **OK**.

4   Click in a cell and type your text. Use the Tab key to navigate from cell to cell.

5   Use buttons on the Tables and Borders toolbar (such as **Merge Cells**, **Split Cells**, **Align**, or **Distribute**) to format and modify the table or individual cells.

To convert existing plain text to a table

1   Select the block of text that you want to convert to a table.

2   On the **Table** menu, point to **Convert** and then click **Text to Table**.

3   Type the number of columns you want to use and then click **OK**.

To sort information in a table

1   Place the insertion point in the column where you want to the sort information.

2   On the **Table** menu, click **Sort**.

3 In the **Sort** dialog box, select the options you want to use and then click **OK**.

To format text in a table

1 In Print Layout view, select the table text that you want to format.

2 Use the Formatting toolbar, the Tables and Borders toolbar and the **Format** menu to make changes to the text and the table.

To format text into columns

1 On the **Format** menu, click **Columns**.

2 In the **Columns** dialog box, type the number of columns you want to use and then click **OK**.

Lesson 6:   Working with Graphics

To insert and modify an organization chart

1 Click in the document to place the insertion point where you want to insert the organization chart.

Insert Diagram or Organization Chart

2 On the Drawing toolbar, click the **Insert Diagram or Organization Chart** button.

3 Click the organization chart icon and then click **OK**.

4 For each entry on the chart, click a text box and then type text.

5 Use the Organization Chart toolbar to modify the organization chart.

To search for, insert and modify clip art

Insert Clip Art

1 On the Drawing toolbar, click the **Insert Clip Art** button.

2 In the **Insert Clip Art** task pane, type a word in the **Search text** box and then click **Search**.

3 In the **Results** list, click a picture and then click the **Close** button to close the **Insert Clip Art** task pane.

4 Drag the sizing handles to resize the picture, if necessary.

5 Use the Picture toolbar to modify the clip art.

To insert and modify a picture

1 Place the insertion point where you want to insert the picture.

2 On the **Insert** menu, point to **Picture** and then click **From File**.

3 Navigate to the file you want to insert and then double-click the picture to insert it.

4 Drag the sizing handles to resize the picture, if necessary.

5 Use the Picture toolbar to modify the picture.

To insert and modify WordArt

Insert WordArt

1   On the Drawing toolbar, click the **Insert WordArt** button.

2   In the **WordArt Gallery** dialog box, click a WordArt style and then click **OK**.

3   In the **Edit WordArt Text** dialog box, type your text and then select the formatting options you want.

4   Click **OK**.

5   Use the WordArt toolbar to modify the object.

Lesson 7:   Working with Charts

To add a chart to a document

1   Click in the document to place the insertion point where you want to add the chart.

2   On the **Insert** menu, point to **Picture** and then click **Chart**.

3   Drag the title bar of the datasheet window so that it is positioned below the sample chart, if necessary.

4   Click the **Select All** button on the datasheet (the upper-left button) and then press Del .

5   Click in the cells and type your text, using the Enter and Tab keys to move from cell to cell.

To modify the appearance of a chart

1   Double-click the chart in the document to activate it.

Chart Type

2   On the Standard toolbar, click the **Chart Type** down arrow and then click a chart type.

3   Use the resize handles on the borders of the chart to modify the size of the chart.

4   Click to select various chart areas and use Graph's Formatting toolbar and menus to modify colour, fills effects, gridlines, legend and other chart items.

Lesson 8:   Collaborating with Others

To merge a document with other versions of the document

1   Open the original document.

2   On the **Tools** menu, click **Compare and Merge Documents**.

3   In the **Compare and Merge Documents** dialog box, navigate to the folder containing other versions of the document.

4   Click the file for another version of the document, click the **Merge** down arrow and then click **Merge into current document**.

To compare merged documents

1   On the Reviewing toolbar, click the **Show** down arrow, point to **Reviewers** and then click one of the reviewers to hide their revisions, click **All Reviewers** to view revisions made by all reviewers, or click **Formatting** to view only insertions and deletions, not formatting changes.

2   Use the Reviewing toolbar to accept or reject tracked changes.

3   On the Reviewing toolbar, click the **Display for Review** down arrow and then click **Final Showing Markup** to view the document with all the revision marks or click **Final** to view the document with all the current changes and without the revision marks.

To show and review comments

Web Layout View

1   Click the **Web Layout View** button to switch to Web Layout view.

2   On the **View** menu, click **Markup** to show comments and changes and to display the Reviewing toolbar.

Next

3   On the Reviewing toolbar, click the **Next** button to display the next comment in the document.

Reviewing Pane

4   On the Reviewing toolbar, click the **Reviewing Pane** button to open the **Reviewing Pane**.

5   Make changes to comments directly in the **Reviewing Pane**.

6   On the Reviewing toolbar, click the **Reviewing Pane** button to close the **Reviewing Pane**.

To add or delete a comment

New Comment

1   On the Reviewing toolbar, click the **New Comment** button.

2   In the comment balloon, type your text.

3   Click a blank area of the document to deselect the comment.

4   To delete a comment, right-click anywhere on text with a comment and then click **Delete Comment**.

Lesson 9:   Working with Documents on the Web

To change Web browser options

1   On the **Tools** menu, click **Options**.

2   Click the **General** tab and then click **Web Options**.

3   Click the **Browser** tab, if necessary, click the **People who view this Web page will be using** down arrow and then click a browser.

4   In the **Options** list, verify that the **Disable features not supported by these browsers** check box is selected and then click **OK** to close the **Web Options** dialog box.

5   Click **OK** to close the **Options** dialog box.

To save a document as a Web page

1   On the **File** menu, click **Save as Web Page**.

2   Navigate to the folder in which you want to save the Web page and then type the file name in the **File name** box.

3   Click the **Save as type** down arrow and then click **Web Page**.

4   Click **Save** and then click **Continue** when the message box appears.

To insert a hyperlink into a document

1   Select the text or object to which you want to add a hyperlink.

Insert Hyperlink

2   On the Standard toolbar, click the **Insert Hyperlink** button.

3   In the **Insert Hyperlink** dialog box, click a file in the list of folders and file names and then click **Target Frame**.

4   Click **OK** to accept the default settings in the **Set Target Frame** dialog box and then click **OK** to close the **Insert Hyperlink** dialog box.

Index

U

V

W

ITS-Feda Ltd
ITS-Feda Ltd is proud to present the Microsoft© Word 2002 Core Skills Student Guide as part of the Microsoft© Office Specialist XP Courseware Series.

The original self-paced training materials created by Perspection Inc., have, thanks to the work of a team of dedicated training professionals and writers, become Microsoft© Office Specialist XP Courseware for Instructor Led, classroom training. This courseware maintains the standards of excellence you have come to expect from ITS-Feda Ltd and Microsoft Press®

The book's straightforward approach and easy to read format provides both the Instructor and the students with the training tool they need to gain the maximum benefit from using Microsoft© Office XP products. The books focus on developing both essential skills and the skills required to pass the Microsoft© Office Specialist Certification Exams.

ITS-Feda Ltd would like to acknowledge the team at TESI Automazione s.r.l. and Microsoft Press® who's hard work has made the production of these materials possible.

For further information please visit our web site at www.itservices.org.uk.

The following materials are also available as part of this range from ITS-Feda Ltd:

Title	ISBN NO.
Word 2002	
Step by Step Courseware: Word Version 2002 Core Skills Student Guide	1-904644-00-7
Step by Step Courseware: Word Version 2002 Expert Skills Student Guide	1-904644-01-5
Step by Step Courseware: Word Version 2002 Instructor Guide	1-904644-02-3
Excel 2002	
Step by Step Courseware: Excel Version 2002 Core Skills Student Guide	1-904644-03-1
Step by Step Courseware: Excel Version 2002 Expert Skills Student Guide	1-904644-04-X
Step by Step Courseware: Excel Version 2002 Instructor Guide	1-904644-05-8
Outlook 2002	
Step by Step Courseware: Outlook Version 2002 Core Skills Student Guide	1-904644-06-6
Step by Step Courseware: Outlook Version 2002 Expert Skills Student Guide	1-904644-07-4
Step by Step Courseware: Outlook Version 2002 Instructor Guide	1-904644-08-2
Access 2002	
Step by Step Courseware: Access Version 2002 Core Skills Student Guide	1-904644-09-0
Step by Step Courseware: Access Version 2002 Expert Skills Student Guide	1-904644-10-4
Step by Step Courseware: Access Version 2002 Instructor Guide	1-904644-11-2
PowerPoint 2002	
Step by Step Courseware: PowerPoint Version 2002 Student Guide	1-904644-12-0
Step by Step Courseware: PowerPoint Version 2002 Instructor Guide	1-904644-13-9

its group

Microsoft Word 2002
Core Exercises
Student

Version 1.0

Table of Contents

SCENARIO FOR EXERCISES

You and three friends have invented a new PC based computer game. You are about to embark on a business venture to get the new game out into the market place. The following are tasks that you have to complete before the bank will grant you a business loan to be able to market the new game.

Important

It is important to complete the exercises in the order of the instructions, as in the exam environment you will be marked down if you complete a question in a different order.

Microsoft Word 2002 Core Chapter 1 Consolidation Exercise

W2002-1-1   Insert modify and move text and symbols

1. Create a new document that looks like the document found on the following page.

   Note: You are not expected to place a border around the text.

2. Let AutoCorrect enter the copyright symbol by typing (c).

3. Move the second paragraph so that it appears just before the line "If I can be of any further assistance...."

4. Move the copyright symbol so that it is placed after the name of the game.

5. Find and replace the text **Personal Computer** with **PC**.

6. Change the postcode to be **BR7 6GA**.

W2002-4-1   Manage files and folders for documents

7. Create a new folder called **Fantasy Games** under the **C:\SBS** folder.

8. Create a new folder under the **C:\SBS\Fantasy Games** folder called **Word**.

9. Create a new folder under the **C:\SBS\Fantasy Games\Word** folder called **Letters**.

W2002-4-3   Save the document in different formats

10. Save the document in the **C:\SBS\Fantasy Games\Word\Letters** folder as **Loan application letter.doc**.

11. Save the document in the **C:\SBS\Fantasy Games\Word\Letters** folder as **Loan application letter v97.doc**, using the correct settings so that someone who uses Microsoft Office 97 would be able to open it.

12. Save the document in the **C:\SBS\Fantasy Games\Word\Letters** folder as **Loan application letter.rtf** in rich text format.

13. Close the rich text version of this document.

14. Open the XP version of the **Loan application letter**.

10 New Road
Pratts Bottom
Kent
BR6 7GA

Dear Sir

With reference to our meeting yesterday concerning the loan application for marketing purposes for the new personal computer game we have created; please find enclosed a copy of our business plan and details of the new game we are planning to market and sell.

The © Castle in the Air game will be aimed at the personal computing market for the age range of 11-16 year olds.

The game is based around a fantasy world, which the players can build, adding fantasy creatures and other equipment the enable them to protect themselves from attack by other online players.

The game is called "Castle In The Air" and we have already applied for copyright for this name.

If I can be of any further assistance please do not hesitate to contact me.

Yours faithfully

Your Name
Sales and Marketing Director
Encl:

Microsoft Word 2002 Core Chapter 2 Consolidation Exercise

W2002-1-5 Enter and format date and time

1. Open the **Loan application letter.doc** file located in the **C:\SBS\Fantasy Games\Word\Letters** folder.

2. Between the Address and the line "Dear Sir" enter today's date using the Date and Time command.

3. Ensure the format for the date shows the weekday and the full month name.

W2002-2-1 Modify paragraph formats

4. Right align the address at the top of the letter.

5. Right align the date.

6. Delete the extra paragraph marks between "Yours faithfully" and "Your name" and add 36 pt spacing before the "Your name" paragraph.

W2002-1-2 Modify and apply text formats

7. Insert a new centred paragraph below "Dear Sir" which is underlined and bold with the following text:
   RE: Loan Application

8. Create an Autotext entry for the complete sentence that starts with "If I can be of any further assistance…", save the entry with the default name.

9. Create an AutoCorrect entry for your name and position, give this Autotext entry your initials as a name.

   Note: If your initials spell a real word, like IS or AM, call the Autotext entry **endlet**.

W2002-1-4 Apply font and text effects

10. Change the font for all the text to **Arial narrow** size **12**.

11. Save the letter in the same folder with the same name.

12. Close the letter.

W2002-2-3 Apply bullet, outline and numbering formats to paragraphs

1. Open the document called **Loan Application Details** from the **C:\SBS\Word\Consolidation\Core** folder.

2. Using bullets outline and numbering to make the document look like the following page.

3. Save the file in a folder called **C:\SBS\Fantasy Games\Word\Loan Application**.

4. Close the document.

Loan Application

This document describes what the loan monies will be used for if the application is approved. It is split into three main sections:

1. Requirements
2. Details
3. Securities

Requirements

This loan is required to enable the Fantasy Games company to be able to:

- Market the new game in time for the Christmas rush
- Employ marketing consultants on a commission basis only
- Advertise the game in a short TV commercial
- Launch the game
- Give away a number of copies as prizes

Details

The following is a breakdown of how the loan monies are to be allocated:

1) **Marketing** **50%**
   a) Consultants 10%
   b) Printing 12%
   c) Packaging 20%
   d) Postage 8%
2) **Launch** **40%**
   a) Advertising 25%
   b) Temporary Staff 10%
   c) Expenses 5%
3) **Competitions** **10%**
   a) Kids TV competition prizes 5%
   b) Computer magazine prizes 5%

Securities

The directors of Fantasy Games will provide security on their properties which matches the loan amount in the following proportions

- Your Name 40%
- Debby Barrington 25%
- Alan Spencer 20%
- Paul Donnachie 15%

These proportions are the same as the proportionate number of shares owned in Fantasy Games.

W2002-2-2   *Set and modify tabs*

1. Open the **Loan application letter v97.doc** document, which can be found in the **C:\SBS\Fantasy Games\Word\Letters** folder.

2. For the whole document, set a right tab at 16cm.

3. Apply this tab to each line of the address and the date.

4. Between the lines "Dear Sir" and the first paragraph add a new line that is bold and underlined as follows:
   RE: Loan Application

   Note: There is a tab before the text **RE** and a space between the colon and the text Loan Application.

5. For this new line create a centre tab that is placed at 6cm.

6. Drag the tab marker in the ruler until the text "RE: Loan Application" looks as if it is in the centre of the page.

7. Change the underline so that only the ext has an underline.

8. Save the document in the same folder with the same name.

   Note: This document should be saved in Word 97 format.

W2002-1-6   *Apply character styles*

1. Open the document called **Loan Application Details** from the **C:\SBS\Fantasy Games\Word\Loan Application** folder.

2. Apply the following character styles as described below:

   Loan Application heading   Title1

   Requirements, Details and Security headings   Title2

3. Save the file with the same name and close it.

Microsoft Word 2002 Core Chapter 3 Consolidation Exercise

W2002-4-2   *Create documents using templates*

1. Create a new Letter using the Fantasy Letter template.

2. Address the letter to:
   Mr Paul Daniels
   Pear Tree Cottage
   Market Lane
   Cheddar Gorge
   CG30 6AB

3. Use the title and last name as the salutation.

4. The subject line is **Design Competition**.

5. The text of the letter should say:

> **Thank you for entering the Design Competition, the standard of designs for the new Castle in the air © Fantasy Games was extremely high.**
>
> **Your design has been chosen as a finalist. As a finalist you are herby invited to attend an award ceremony, at the Hilton hotel in London.**
>
> **All finalists will receive a copy of the Castle in the air © game, and the winner will also see their design being used as the image on the game's CD and the packaging.**
>
> **The winning designers name will also appear on the external packaging for the game.**
>
> **Your invitation to this event should arrive within two weeks. If you have not received the invitation after three weeks from the date of this letter, please contact the Competition winners hotline on 0870 7447367.**

6. End the letter with your name and position, **Sales and Marketing Director**.

7. Save the letter in the **C:\SBS\Fantasy Games\Word\Letters** folder as **Invitation for Competition Winner Paul Daniels 2004.doc**.

8. Close the letter.

W2002-3-1 *Create and modify headers and footers.*

1. Open the letter in the **C:\SBS\Fantasy Games\Word\Letters** folder called **Invitation for Competition Winner Paul Daniels 2004.doc**

2. In the header for your letter add the following address aligned to the right, as: Arial, font size 12, Bold.

   Fantasy Games
   10 New Road
   Pratts Bottom
   Kent
   BR7 6GA

3. Edit the footer of this letter to include a page number prefixed by the word **Page** and aligned to the right.

4. Save the letter as the same name.

5. Close the document.

W2002-3-3 *Modify document layout and Page Setup options*

1. Open the document called **Winners Invitation**, which can be found in the **C:\SBS\Word\Consolidation\Core** folder.

2. Make the following changes to this document:

   a. Change the paper size to A5 with Landscape orientation.

   b. Change all the margins to be 2 cm.

   c. Set Vertical Layout to Centre.

   d. Set Page Border as **Gold Stars**

3. Save the document as the same name in the **C:\SBS\Fantasy Games\Word\Letters** folder.

W2002-3-5 *Apply paragraph styles*

1. Apply the **Invitation** style to the text "Winners Invitation".

2. Apply the **RSVP** style to the last two paragraphs of the invitation.

3. Save the document.

4. Delete the line of dots and enter the name **Mr Paul Daniels**.

5. Format the text **Mr Paul Daniels** as **Monotype Corsiva** size **16**.

6. Save the document to the same folder with the name **Winners Invitation to Paul Daniels**.

7. Close the document.

Microsoft Word 2002 Core Chapter 4 Consolidation Exercise

W2002-3-5 *Preview and print documents envelopes and labels*

1. Open the document called **Invitation for Competition Winner Paul Daniels 2004.doc**, which can be found in the **C:\SBS\Fantasy Games\Word\Letters** folder.

2. Preview the letter and print it.

3. Print a label for the letter using the Avery A4 and A5 standard label called L7551. The next label that can be used on the sheet is on the second row in the first column.

4. Add a C5 envelope for the **Competition Winner Paul Daniels 2004.doc** letter to the document.

5. Save the letter with the same name and close it.

6. Open the **Winners Invitation to Paul Daniels** document, preview it and then print it.

7. Close the file.

W2002-1-3 *Correct spelling and grammar usage*

1. Open the document called **Letter to K Potts about missing instructions.doc**, which can be found in the **C:\SBS\Word\Consolidation\Core** folder.

2. Run the spell checker on this document and correct spelling and grammar as necessary.

Note: When correcting the spelling, add the incorrectly spelt word **receving** and its correct spelling to Autocorrect.

3. Save the document with the same name in the **C:\SBS\Fantasy Games\Word\Letters** folder

Microsoft Word 2002 Core Chapter 5 Consolidation Exercise

W2002-3-2   Apply and modify column settings

1. Open the document called **Instructions** from the **C:\SBS\Word\Consolidation\Core** folder.

2. Change the page layout to Landscape.

3. Apply an even 3-column format to the whole document.

4. Add a next page section break after the paragraph that says "Graphic to go in here".

5. Vertically centre the first section.

6. Place a column break after each of the following points:

   a. The end of the address

   b. Table to be entered here text

   c. The last requirement

   d. The Good Luck message

7. Remove the bullet point on the blank line before **How to Play**.

8. Save the document in a new folder as follows:

   C:\SBS\Fantasy Games\Word\Instructions
   Trifold with comments.doc

W2002-3-4   Create and modify tables

1. Create the following table in the **Trifold with comments.doc** document replacing the text "**Table to be entered here**".

Description	Key 1	Key 2
New Game	Alt	N
New Item	Ctrl	N
Open	Ctrl	O
Save	Ctrl	S
Copy	Ctrl	C
Cut	Ctrl	X
Paste	Ctrl	V
Properties	Shift	F4
Help	F1	

2. Save the document with the same name.

Microsoft Word 2002 Core Chapter 6 Consolidation Exercise

W2002-5-1   *Insert images and graphics*

1. Search for a picture of a castle.

   Note: Castle graphics can be found in the
   C:\SBS\Word\Consolidation\Core folder.

2. Replace the text **Graphic to go in here** by inserting a graphic that you like.

3. Change the text above the graphic to be Word Art.

   Note: The graphic and WordArt need to stay in one column.

4. Save and close the file.

W2002-5-2   *Create and modify diagrams and charts*

1. In a new blank document create an organisation chart that shows the following staff details:

Name	Position	Reports to
Your Name	Managing Director / Sales and Marketing Director	
Paul Donnachie	Customer Services Director	Managing Director
Alan Spencer	Development Director	Managing Director
Paul Gallagher	Senior Programmer	Development Director
Debby Barrington	Finance Director	Managing Director
Mike Lewis	Accountant	Finance Director

2. Save the document in the **C:\SBS\Fantasy Games\Word\Company Information** folder with the title of **Organisation Chart.doc**.

3. Close the document.

Microsoft Word 2002 Core Chapter 7 Consolidation Exercise

W2002-5-2   Create and modify diagrams and charts

1. Create a new blank document.

2. Using the Heading 1 style give the page the title of **Loan Application Allocation**.

3. Insert a 3-D Pie Chart in this document using the following information.

Description	Percentage
Consultants	10%
Printing	12%
Packaging	20%
Postage	8%
Advertising	25%
Temporary Staff	10%
Expenses	5%
Kids TV competition prizes	5%
Computer magazine prizes	5%

4. Save the document as **Loan Application Allocation Chart.doc** in the **C:\SBS\Fantasy Games\Word\Loan Application** folder.

5. Change the colours in the pie chart to patterns, as you will be printing to a black and white printer.

6. Save the file into the **C:\SBS\Fantasy Games\Word\Loan Application** folder, with the name **B&W Loan Application Allocation Chart.doc**.

7. Close the document.

Microsoft Word 2002 Core Chapter 8 Consolidation Exercise

W2002-6-2   Insert View and edit comments

1. Open the document called **Trifold instructions for review.doc**, which can be found in the **C:\SBS\Word\Consolidation\Core** folder.

2. Enter the following comments in relevant positions:

   a. The copyright sign should be on the same line as the name of the game.

   b. Should we put age and gender on the same line?

   c. Move the bullets across for the How to Play section.

   d. Move the outline level 2 letters across.

   e. 1.8 GHz of what, should we say processing speed?

3. Save the document as **Trifold instructions with comments.doc** in the **C:\SBS\Fantasy Games\Word\Instructions** folder.

4. Close the document.

5. Open the document called **Trifold instructions.doc**, which can be located in the **C:\SBS\Word\Consolidation\Core** folder.

6. View the comments made on this document, do not delete any of the comments.

7. Save this document with the same name into the **C:\SBS\Fantasy Games\Word\Instructions** folder.

W2002-6-1   Compare and merge documents

1. Open the document called
   Trifold instructions with comments.doc and merge it with the document called **Trifold instructions reviewed.doc**, which can be located in the **C:\SBS\Word\Consolidation\Core** folder.

2. Review the changes and accept all the changes individually.

3. Save the document with the name
   Trifold instructions merged.doc in the
   C:\SBS\Fantasy Games\Word\Instructions folder.

4. Ensure that Track Changes is turned on.

5. Action all the comments that are outstanding.

6. Delete all comments.

7. Save the document with the same name.

Microsoft Word 2002 Core Chapter 9 Consolidation Exercise

W2002-6-3 Convert documents into web pages

1. Open the file called **Instructions for the web.doc**, which can be found in the **C:\SBS\Word\Consolidation\Core** folder.

2. Create a "Mailto" hyperlink on the email address **info@fantasygames.fslife.co.uk**.

3. Create hyperlinks to the **Installation Instructions**, **Requirements** and **How to play** sections from the bulleted list at the beginning of the document.

4. Save the file as a web page with the same name in the **C:\SBS\Fantasy Games\Word\Instructions** folder.

5. View the document using Internet Explorer.

6. Close the document.